trials by wildfire

in search of the
new warrior spirit

Peter M. Leschak

Pfeifer-Hamilton Publishers
Duluth, Minnesota

Other titles by Peter M. Leschak

Letters from Side Lake *The Bear Guardian*
Bumming with the Furies *Seeing the Raven*
Hellroaring   *The Snow Lotus*
Rogues and Toads

Portions of this book originally appeared in *Astronomy Magazine,*
The Fireman's Journal, Mpls/St. Paul Magazine, National Fire and Rescue,
and *Wildfire Magazine.*

Pfeifer-Hamilton Publishers
210 W Michigan
Duluth MN 55802-1908
218-727-0500 www.phpublisher.com

Trials by Wildfire: In Search of the New Warrior Spirit
© 2000 by Peter M. Leschak. All rights reserved.
Except for short excerpts for review purposes, no part of this book may be
reproduced by any means, electronic or mechanical, including photocopy-
ing, without permission in writing from the publisher.

Printed in the United States of America by Versa Press, Inc.
10 9 8 7 6 5 4 3 2 1

Cover Photo: © 1995 by Tom Storey
Cover Design: Jerry Lehman
Editorial Director: Heather Isernhagen
Art Director: Joy Morgan Dey

Library of Congress Cataloging-in-Publication Data

Leschak, Peter M., 1951–
 Trials by wildfire : in search of the new warrior spirit
/ by Peter Leschak
  176 p. 23 cm.
 ISBN 1-57025-198-3 (pbk.)
 1. Forest fires—Prevention and control Ancedotes. 2. Forest firefighters
Anecdotes. 3. Leschak, Peter M., 1951– I. Title.
 SD421.233 .L47 2000
 363.37'9—dc21
       99-6690
       CIP

For all those who carry their gear

Acknowledgments

Thanks to the crew at Pfeifer-Hamilton for their validation and good work, and to editor Pat C. West at National Fire and Rescue for providing opportunities and encouragement, and not least to all those—too numerous to mention—who taught me how to carry my gear.

Contents

I like to have a man's knowledge comprehend more than one class of topics, one row of shelves. I like a man who likes to see a fine barn as well as a good tragedy.

Ralph Waldo Emerson

The greatest and most important problems of life are all fundamentally insoluble. They can never be solved but only outgrown.

Carl Jung

The gods love the obscure and hate the obvious.

The Upanishads

WHISTLE

On a sweltering day in late February 1972, I volunteered for a search party. An old man had been missing for two days, and the authorities requested help. The east Texas woods were tangled and mean, and it seemed that every vine brandished thorns, every hollow sheltered venomous snakes. There were scorpions. I've tramped more congenial country.

My buddy Ron and I were skirting the bank of a sluggish creek when he whistled. There was a screen of dense foliage between us and I said, "What is it?"

He whistled again.

"Yeah, what?"

A pause. Then Ron's voice cracked a reply, "What do you think!"

He'd found the old man—damn near tripped over the dead feet.

I pushed through the brush and for the first time in adult life saw a human corpse that wasn't manicured and casketed. The old man was face-down in Big Sandy Creek and already bloated. The toes of his shoes clung to the muddy bank.

Ron and I stared in silence. I had not expected to find the old man—dead or alive—I'd joined the search impulsively. But there he was. I felt both revulsion and triumph. We found him. But already he was the color of the creek bottom, looked as if he belonged to it. Looked as if he'd bloomed like gray-brown algae. Crayfish food.

That scene comes to mind often, though after all these years, not morbidly. I remember Ron's whistle. His vocal chords were paralyzed with shock, and all he could do was force breath through his teeth. It was a summons: come see death, I've discovered it here.

In those days a popular proverb appeared on posters, buttons, T-shirts: "Today is the first day of the rest of your life." It was ubiquitous, like an atmospheric gas, and soon taken for granted. I don't recall ever discussing its meaning or implication with anyone, though it gave me pause the first time I saw it. I rendered the most obvious interpretation: you can change who and what you are, you're not dead yet, so forge a new beginning. Or something like that. Whiffs of grapeshot scented the air. Cultural revolution. We could all be made over, reborn—and I sensed in the proverb and in the times an injunction that we all should be reborn.

Recognizing the potential of each fresh morning is not a bad outlook, but as I stood over the old man's decaying body the obvious corollary seemed more compelling: each day could also be my last.

Although we needed to announce our discovery, I hesitated to shout in the presence of the corpse, as if the old man would be disturbed, perhaps even awaken and rise. Didn't want that. Ron and I were as still as the mud, and I realized that he'd been temporarily muted not only by shock, but also by reluctance to speak near the body. A whistle was less obtrusive, akin to the bird calls we'd heard all morning and not likely to arouse. Weird, but somehow proper.

"Death," wrote W. H. Auden, "is the sound of distant thunder at a picnic." And that's the customary mode of our apprehension: yes, yes, we'll die someday (I guess), but no need to dwell on it; have another hot dog; after all, it is distant thunder.

The bloated man was not an angelic spectacle, but after the initial scare neither was he horrific. Sad, certainly, but less so than a dead child would've been. Most of all, the old man was fascinating. Partly the sheer novelty of it—a majority of Americans don't stumble across corpses every day—but mainly it was his altered state. This man had accomplished the ineluctable transformation from the living to the dead. He was beyond pleasure and pain, had transcended desire and care. He nurtured no hope, harbored no fear. His existence was magnificently simplified, his future course clarified—dissolution, recycling into the earth and atmosphere. Today was the first day of the end of his life. Every day for everyone promises such potential.

That's what I formally remind myself in the morning: I could be dead by sundown. It hammers my obligations and ambitions into perspective. Think about it, I say: you could die before noon. It is not a macabre obsession. A deliberate awareness of death allows each day to be viewed (if only briefly) as the last opportunity. In that context it is useless to worry; self-pity or whining are impotent, ludicrous. It makes sense to strive for the best, do good work, and go out in style if need be.

I am more fortunate than many because on my chosen trail through life I still meet untreated corpses from time to time. Occasionally I help to lift and carry them away. It's not cheerful duty, but it's worthy labor that helps to reinforce my appreciation of death. As a firefighter, I'm often able to sweep away the cluttering gimcrack of petty concerns. At a fire, a car wreck, or other emergency, it's easier to be focused beyond the grasping self. After the incident, it seems appropriate to shun nagging trifles that can mutate into tempests in teapots. Such storms sap energy, waste time, and over the long haul, tend to hasten dying. If you seek to enhance life, it's smart to acknowledge death—regularly.

Ron found the old man around midday, with the sun high, bright, and deceptively forthcoming. I prefer to recognize mortality in twilight, at dusk or dawn, awash in a vulpecular blend of radiance and shadow, and with T. S. Eliot,

> *Wavering between the profit and the loss*
> *In this brief transit where the dreams cross*
> *The dream-crossed twilight between birth*
> *and dying.*

Everyone faces a "twilight struggle" sometime, an episode where there are few straight and level paths, no easy solutions, where allies and enemies dress in shades of gray, and doubled-edged swords are all that can be wielded.

The single indisputable human truth is that we all perish. Death is therefore a beacon. The old man was a prophet. Ron and I were disciples. Ron had to whistle because he didn't have a cornet. His whistle was a fanfare.

This book is about the warrior code. By warrior I do not mean the macho, Rambo-with-bandoleers cartoon figure, but the warrior of the spirit. The code celebrates struggle more than outcome, and is exemplified by will, patience, integrity, courage, responsibility, and commitment. It is male and female in character.

I will not preach about the code. I'm a storyteller—no more, no less—and we'll explore the warrior spirit via narrative. Many of the stories are about firefighting because, (1) it's what I know best, (2) it provides compelling tales and settings, and (3) firefighting is an elemental kind of struggle that provides apt analogy and metaphor to highlight the warrior code. And as is life itself, firefighting is dangerous, sometimes leading to early death.

The warrior is conscious of death—I mean truly aware on a daily basis. This is not morbid. It's a healthy acknowledgment of reality that helps to focus the intellect and the emotions. To quote a popular song: Don't worry, be happy. You can do nothing about your ultimate fate on this planet, so live well. Make a good and worthy life. If need be, whistle. If death is a loss, then we all lose the battle. So the best we can do is mount a good fight. A fair fight.

My true stories are not all fire and fury. There are boreal forest afternoons, the night sky, the music of bagpipes, and the intricacies of an ancient Chinese board game. We'll bask in the warm fellowship of a small town tavern. We'll admire the flight of ravens. The warrior relishes all of life, and that includes, if possible, the final passage.

I think it's important to tell you that I was born in 1951. If you are a student of history, current events, and human nature—and most of us are to one degree or another—then that one fact tells you a lot about me. It also shows that I am not yet old. I am not yet suffering from a terminal illness. I'm fit and available for dispatch. Why you should know this will become evident as you read the following stories.

The dispatchers at the Minnesota Interagency Fire Center (MIFC) in Grand Rapids are aware that when it comes to fire assignments my motto is "anytime, anywhere." And that, dear reader, is where I intend to take you.

CHAPTER ONE

The Witness Post

I was so much older then
I'm younger than that now.

Bob Dylan

I drew up a living will because of U Thant. A statement made by
the former secretary general of the United Nations in the tense
ambience of 1968 has hung with me like the memory of a dead
puppy—warm and fuzzy riding a jagged glass edge.

On Christmas Eve 1968 I slouched in one of my mother's
front-room chairs—I always thought of the furniture as hers—
and stared at the Christmas tree in the far corner. It was past midnight; the rest of the family was asleep. I was seventeen years old
and nurturing an adolescent sensation of being misplaced, forfeit.
I knew I was no longer a child because the winking colored lights
and tinsel left me unmoved, actually seemed to mock the deep
shadows that had pinched off a brief glimmer of holiday cheer.
The mound of packages beneath the tree looked like kindling,
inviting the flare of a kitchen match.

I had attended midnight Mass at St. Joseph's with my mother and two siblings, and that normally soothing spectacle was merely grating. All I could focus on was the giant crucifix behind the altar and the dead face of Jesus Christ carved in dark wood. I was doomed—I could see that clearly, even through a haze of incense.

Nineteen-sixty-eight had scared me. Martin Luther King Jr. and Bobby Kennedy were assassinated; Paul Erlich's apocalyptic warning *The Population Bomb* hit the streets; civil unrest, particularly in Paris and at the Democratic Convention in Chicago, was rampant; Nixon edged out Hubert Humphery, a huge local favorite, in the presidential election; the Soviets invaded Czechoslovakia, emphasizing the East-West tension that to my mind made global nuclear war inevitable—perhaps only a few years away.

When I imagined the future, it looked like that hardwood face of Christ, only incinerated in the maelstrom of atomic holocaust. After all, Secretary General U Thant, a person who would know (one would think), said in 1968 that he figured the world had only a decade to change its ways or court destruction. He may have intended his words as instructive hyperbole, but I believed him.

Even pop music had taken a turn for the funereal. I was a devoted listener of WEBC, the rock station out of Duluth, and earlier in the winter they had started playing the mournful tune "Abraham, Martin, and John," a song that attempted the impossible: to be an upbeat dirge for murder victims. It referred to Lincoln, King, and the dead Kennedys, the latter not yet a moniker for a heavy metal band. The record made people shake their heads in communal remorse—for the dead, for the nation, for the sappy song itself.

At midnight Mass the choir had sung a rousing version of what I called "Gloria," the hymn that starts "Angels we have heard on high . . . " and builds to the stirring Latin chorus that seemed to ring off the stained glass and airy vault of St. Joseph's. Those echoes had inspired the fleeting spark of Christmas spirit, but ultimately were no musical match for "Abraham, Martin, and John." That tune was stubbornly lodged in my brain. Those men had been doomed, we were doomed, I was doomed.

And of course there was Vietnam. The Tet Offensive—in January and February of '68—had been a shock, a true Pyrrhic victory for the Americans and the South Vietnamese. For almost five years, while working my newspaper route, I'd watched the war mutate and evolve on the front page of the *Hibbing Daily Tribune*—from the relative innocence of the Tonkin Gulf incident to the blood rivers of Tet and beyond. In a few months I would be eighteen years old and out of high school, possibly facing conscription into the armed forces of the United States, possibly sentenced to the carnage in Southeast Asia. I was doomed.

Our Christmas tree had always been a surrogate campfire to me, a warm and cheery flambeau at the darkest, and often coldest nadir of the Minnesota winter. It was a cornucopia of color and gifts; the much anticipated annual ritual of decorating it transformed the prosaic front room with light, reflections, and the heady fragrance of spruce or fir. But on that Christmas Eve, downwind from the noxious pall that was 1968, and racked by the doubt and alienation that encompasses age seventeen in America, I decided I was gazing at my last Christmas tree.

Suicide. At least I could wrest some control from doom. The method seemed obvious, foolproof. Next spring I would enlist in the Army or Marine Corps and volunteer for combat duty in Vietnam. Dying there should be simple, and no one at home need know it was intentional. I would be remembered not as a failure (and sinner), but as a fallen hero; at worst, a tragic victim of history. I could live with that, so to speak.

I remember my mind being made up, not unlike a bed—all tidy and smoothed over with the corners tucked in. It was satisfying to have an unambiguous goal.

A few months later I encountered a poem written during World War I by William Butler Yeats. To me, *An Irish Airman Foresees*

His Death was both a tonic and a lash. I was astounded that a foreign poet who had been in his grave for thirty years could have so infallibly plumbed my psyche in verse written over half a century before. I was not yet aware how closely the general human experience is mimicked in individual lives and how relatively few are the plot lines available for us to play out. But Yeats's point and impression were made, and I christened him a genius. The poem instantly resonated—a *con motto* performance in my head—and I memorized it. It was something I needed to carry, like a totem, and it seemed to bless my resolve of Christmas Eve 1968. It began:

> *I know that I shall meet my fate*
> *Somewhere in the clouds above;*
> *Those that I fight I do not hate,*
> *Those that I guard I do not love;*

Yes, I would seek a sure end in the culturally approved mayhem of war. In years to come, in memories and on monuments, such a death would take on the aura of liturgy. And how true it was that I did not hate the Viet Cong and North Vietnamese, any more than I loved the South Vietnamese. These people were not the point.

> *My country is Kiltartan Cross*
> *My countrymen Kiltartan's poor,*
> *No likely end could bring them loss*
> *Or leave them happier than before.*

In the hearts and minds of the American public and Minnesota neighbors, the termination of my teenaged life would be insignificant. It would alter nothing of importance one way or the other. Family and friends would be affected, of course, but my presence would naturally fade, and besides, *they* were all doomed as well.

Nor law, nor duty bade me fight
Nor public men, nor cheering crowds,
A lonely impulse of delight
Drove me to this tumult in the clouds.

There was law—administered by the Selective Service System—
and a backdrop of implied duty and political rhetoric, but none
of that influenced my decision. In 1966, for example, in a tenth-
grade biology class, the instructor (who was a World War II veteran) had told the boys that we would soon have "our chance" at
war. He seemed curiously satisfied with the notion, but I was only
suspicious and skeptical. No, it was the bittersweet glow of the
Christmas tree and the perceived desolation of adolescence in 1968
that caused my pulse to stutter when I first read *"A lonely impulse
of delight"* and vigorously highlighted it in red ink. That was how
I would face death and "the tumult," and I spun out fantasies of
heroism and glory for the final chapter of my mercifully abbrevi-
ated life.

I balanced all, brought all to mind,
The years to come seemed waste of breath,
A waste of breath the years behind
In balance with this life, this death.

Exactly. What, of any substance, could be accomplished in the
few years remaining to human civilization, and what was so great
about it, or me, anyway? Better to quickly channel the dark flow
of inevitable doom. At least "this death" supported a veneer of
romance.

The next night, after a tedious Christmas Day spent in mandatory association with a less than favorite relative, I slung my
hockey stick and skates over my shoulder and walked the four
blocks to the public rink. Since it was a holiday, no warming-
shack attendant was on duty, and the floodlights were off. The

rink was deserted. The night was biting cold—below zero—but I sat on the ice and pulled on my skates, fingers going numb with the lacing and tying.

I humped around the darkened rink, slamming a puck against the boards and into empty nets. I worked hard, surging for warmth, and trying to shake the overfed holiday blahs.

When I felt sweat on my back, I paused in the middle of the ice sheet, as lonely as a lost child. There was no delight. The only impulse was to unleash another furious slap shot, or perhaps to lie down on the ice until overcome by the final sleep.

It was melodramatic self-pity, of course, all of it. But such can kill. My intention to die was sincere, and I believe I would have followed the model of Yeats's Irish Airman. I wonder how many of my cohort did?

But my scheme to join the military was sidetracked by conversion to a fundamentalist Christian sect that forbade such intimate participation in human affairs.* I threw away a large portion of my book collection. Along with dozens of science fiction novels (considered frivolous and evil), I also discarded a pound or so of recruitment brochures I'd picked up at the post office. Suddenly I was a pacifist, and entered training for the ministry—God's army. I legally avoided the draft, finally pulling a high lottery number, and did not meet my fate in Vietnam.

But in my book of Yeats's poetry, the Irish Airman still foresees his death, and I can yet recite the words. It is a key to remembrance, a portrait of a young man on Christmas Eve 1968. In a way, that young man is indeed dead, altered beyond recognition by three decades of living and the dreamy tides of recollection and wishes.

In his book *Sand and Foam*, Kahlil Gibran wrote a prose poem that encapsulates the pitfalls of memory and desire:

---

*See my book *Bumming with the Furies*, North Star Press, 1993.

*Seven centuries ago seven white doves rose from a
deep valley flying to the snow white summit of the
mountain. One of the seven men who watched the
flight said, "I see a black spot on the wing of the
seventh dove." Today the people in that valley tell
of seven black doves that flew to the summit of the
snowy mountain.*

Perception is tricky.

That's why, when this country was mapped by the United States
Coast and Geodetic Survey, their surveyors established bench-
marks—permanent reference points that are marked by small brass
badges set in concrete near ground level. Such triangulation sta-
tions can be used again and again to help update maps and confirm boundaries. But a benchmark is useless unless it can be found,
and so they are often advertised by a "witness post."

Not far from my present home stands an old fire lookout tower,
and just behind it is a benchmark that was established in 1947. A
foot and a half to the east a short metal post bears a rusting rectangular sign that reads:

WITNESS POST
Please Do Not Disturb Nearby Survey Marker

A few weeks ago, when I first conjured up Christmas Eve 1968,
canvassing both memory and journal entries, I realized that *An
Irish Airman Foresees His Death* was such a witness post. The poem
signaled a benchmark in my life, a survey marker indicating who
I was and who I am—the boundaries of the self. The poem/post
remains intact, and the nearby survey marker of Christmas Eve
1968 remains etched and usable. Recently it helped spur me to
positive action.

For about five years the forms and instruction booklet for a
living will and health care declaration gathered dust on a corner

of my desk. It was one of those good ideas/good intentions that just never jelled.

But in an odd moment, which regrettably has no witness post of its own, the '68 death wish, the Yeats poem, and the warning from U Thant all coalesced in memory. I realized the story was incomplete, the business of parrying fate unfinished. I required fresh resolve, and that resolve needed to reflect nearly three decades of "the years behind" and whatever may be of "years to come." U Thant's warning to the planet is obviously musty, but for each individual it carries the weight of inevitability. I am still doomed. Thant himself left the world in 1974, and I hope he was prepared.

The preparation of my will and declaration seemed morbid at first, all the talk of terminal injury and illness, vegetative states, insurance policies, and funeral arrangements, but by the end of the process I felt the relief and release of establishing another witness post—this one for the final benchmark. It's an image of the decision made in 1968, with a key difference: it is *notarized*.

"I know that I shall meet my fate . . . "

Of course, but it seems OK now. I have witnesses.

CHAPTER TWO

The Fire Tower

That in my action I may soar as high
As I can now discern with this clear eye.

Henry David Thoreau

On a parched, gusty afternoon in late May I jogged up the 126 wooden steps of the Side Lake fire tower. Almost immediately I spotted a gray-black puff of smoke surging out of the forest about ten miles to the south. The wind flattened it out of sight amidst the distant foliage, but I had a fix.

I rushed down the steps, palms buffing smooth steel guardrails polished by thousands of human hands for over fifty years. Even in my haste to report a fire, I relished the moment when I breached the forest canopy, descending below the tree tops like a blue jay banking for a jackpine branch. This tree-top/sky interface is even more dramatic on the way up, always tinged with suspense. What marvel will be revealed when I rise above the last terminal buds into the aerie of a 360-degree horizon?

Once I saw yellow mist drifting out of a pine grove and over Perch Lake, and thought at first it was some kind of weird smoke. Then I made the connection between the trees and the date—

June 3—and realized it was pine pollen, released by the wind and burgeoning into veritable clouds of male reproductive dust. From the tower it appeared as thick as fog.

But on that May afternoon it was smoke I had seen, and once on the ground I trotted across the road to the forestry office and informed my boss we had a fire. I jabbed an index finger to a spot on the wall-mounted survey map.

"There, close to Five Corners."

"OK, head that way."

My engine crew and I hustled to our one-ton Type-6 fire rig, and as we wheeled out of the station we heard the boss call Hibbing dispatch over the radio to report the smoke. The area detection aircraft, Aero-1, was already orbiting a fire near Eveleth, and dispatch asked the observer to take a look back in our direction. She did.

"Hibbing, this is Aero-1. All I see is dust off the mine dumps."

The wind was indeed kicking up loose tailings and overburden—I'd seen it from the tower. But I had also seen smoke, I was sure of it. I kept driving south, and the boss requested that the Deer River Area detection plane—Alpha-22—which was nearby, take a swing over the Five Corners neighborhood and check it out.

The radio frequency we were using was boosted on the Side Lake repeater, working off an antenna affixed to the fire tower. That's the chief reason the tower still stands—a radio link. Most fire detection duties in Minnesota are now handled via air patrols, and towers have supposedly been rendered obsolete. We were testing that assertion.

I first climbed the Side Lake tower in the summer of 1963. I was twelve years old and had never flown in an airplane. The cupola of the fire tower was the highest I'd ever been, and the view was mind-expanding. For the first time I plainly comprehended the versant of the place where I lived, could genuinely appreciate the lay of the land. I suddenly understood a simple, implicit notion that until then had been academic knowledge:

land sheds water, and no matter how convoluted the terrain, the water all flows to the same place. Stunningly obvious? Yes, precisely—obvious in the manner of all youthful revelations.

Just last year I was paddling on a river toward a lake; that is, the river emptied into the lake. Clear? I was with three intelligent, well-educated companions, and was startled when one asked, "How do you know we're going the right way?" At first I didn't understand the question; then I realized I had long ago internalized the concept of "downstream," with direction of flow as infallible guide.

Likewise, from the fire tower I'd traced the drainages and noted the slopes—in juxtaposition with the sparkling surfaces of four lakes and a glint of the river that led the way to the Canadian border and eventually Hudson Bay. The shape of the local watershed is the ancient spoor of an Ice Age glacier, and I could understand it from the tower, could see the deep "rift" of Pickeral Lake, the water hidden by steep ridges studded with mature red pine; on the northwest horizon the bumpy moraines and drumlins of the McCarthy Beach State Park hiking trails; just to the north, the depressions in the forest denoting a pair of kettle lakes. From the tower I defined "home turf"—in space, time, and shape.

As we sped south on County Highway 5, searching the horizon for smoke, Alpha-22 was approaching my estimated position for the fire. The observer radioed Side Lake and said, "I see a lot of dust off the mine dumps, but that's all."

I was chilled by doubt. Could that gray-black puff have been tailings dust, or perhaps a plume of road dust raised by a truck on a gravel road? No. It was smoke, bet my paycheck on it. And there were higher stakes: I had a reputation to uphold, not only as a denizen of the fire tower, but as Smokey Bear himself.

I often don one of the DNR's Hollywood-made Smokey Bear suits and participate in fire awareness/prevention programs for school children. I don't receive higher pay for being a star, and in warm weather the heavy costume is stifling, but there are rewards:

the rapturous expressions of kindergartners as a jovial Smokey ambles into their classroom; the enthusiastic high-fives of jaded eighth graders who still implicitly trust the image of a bear that's never been commercialized, never tried to sell them jeans, ranger hats, or fire extinguishers; the warm handshakes of teachers and parents who are still bemused after all these years; and of course the unexpected lessons—like the incident in front of the fire tower.

One spring day the foresters hosted a class of preschoolers at the Side Lake station, and Smokey—that is, I—was part of the event. After being snugly zipped into the suit, I hid in the woods behind the fire tower, a handheld radio clutched in my paw. When the kids arrived, a forester had one of them call me on the radio, and when I replied in a jolly ursine *basso profundo,* I heard them squeal in delight from a hundred yards away. Since visibility is marginal from inside the costume, I cautiously picked my way down a forest path, each footfall slow and calculated. Our plan was to have Smokey emerge from the woods in front of the fire tower, thus vividly associating all three—the trees, the bear, the tower. But to meet the adoring children in the station parking lot, I then had to cross County Highway 5, a sometimes busy road supporting its share of rumbling pulp haulers. It's not difficult to picture a gold mine of tabloid images concerning Smokey Bear as roadkill—the spiffy ranger hat plastered to the grill of a logging truck.

So when I reached the shoulder of the highway I stopped. To adequately peer out the eye holes, I turned my entire body to the south, then swiveled to the north. From across the road I heard a mother preach: "Did you see that, Amanda? See how Smokey looks both ways before he crosses the road?" Right on, lady, this bear is no fool.

In the engine on that afternoon in May, my fear was growing that what radio communications had by then dubbed "Pete's smoke" was in fact dust and that subsequent ribbing would span the rest of my career. We were also tying up a detection aircraft and, not least, besmirching the character of my esteemed fire tower.

I had just turned the engine around for a slow, uncertain cruise back north when Alpha-22 radioed Side Lake: "I've spotted the fire."

I whooped, switched on our beacon, and gunned the engine. The fire was only three miles away, and definitely in the area I'd indicated from the tower. A few minutes later we pulled up to where wind had toppled a balsam fir across a powerline and ignited grass and brush on the ground. The puff of dark smoke I'd seen was probably the brief initial torching of the resinous fir itself, and I was lucky to have spotted it at all.

But the fire tower was vindicated, and I was grateful for the privilege of being able to climb it and to scan horizons for smoke—or pollen, or eagles—or just to admire the lay of the land.

A couple of years ago the tower assumed a new role for me—gymnasium. Those 126 steps, rapidly scaled six times in twenty minutes, became the core of my daily workout.

Because of my fire-fighting vocation, I'm a fanatic about fitness—have to be, I'm too old to fake it. This was pointedly demonstrated during the wilderness fires in the Boundary Waters Canoe Area in the summer of 1995. I was introducing myself to a young firefighter when he interrupted: "Oh, I know you."

"Yeah?"

"Yeah. You graduated from high school with my mother."

Yeah? Great. At age forty-six, only relentless toil will keep me in the game with the young bucks. And a half-dozen quick "laps" up and down the fire tower is serious toil. My starting pulse rate might be 72 beats per minute. By the time I hustle to the top, the rate can surge to 156. I measure recovery rate—the telling stat—before I hurry down to scuff a lap tally in the dirt and do a couple of pull-ups on an angle-iron cross beam.

One late-September afternoon I performed my ascents, then rested in the cupola. It was sixty-two degrees and sunny, one of

those transcendent autumn days that makes me shout at the sky—
"Yes!" Only that: "Yes!"

From the tower I could see the maples had turned, glowing in
fierce shades of red and orange amidst the deep green of the conifers and the diffused yellow of aspen and birch that were just beginning the metamorphosis. A silken breeze rustled the forest
canopy far below, and I smelled the season—crisp and tart, dry
and cool—like a blend of distant wood smoke and the pungent
aroma of fresh chanterelles.

I gazed at the scenery until my pulse was near normal, then
started down the stairs. I kept an eye out for inscriptions I hadn't
noticed before. The steps, rails, and superstructure of the tower
are crammed with names and dates going back to the 1930s. Some
were scratched into wood or steel with knife blades, but most
were penciled in, and I'm amazed at the durability of graphite on
metal. "J. P. May 18, 1952" is as legible as the new generation of
scribblings from the '90s. I've smiled to note that local people
who are now grandparents left their marks thirty-five years ago,
to be followed by their children a decade and a half later, and
eventually, no doubt, by their grandchildren—genealogical graf-
fiti. As a monument, the fire tower is an irresistible tablet. And
yes, I've done my part.

From the top flight to the first landing I spotted several familiar inscriptions, but as I turned to descend the second flight, I
froze. I stood and gaped. There was a name and date I hadn't seen.
It wasn't new, and it occupied a prominent location. I couldn't
believe I hadn't noticed it. Only the day before I'd heard that Jack,
a childhood playmate a year younger than I, had died of cancer.
My mother gave me the grim details: he'd suffered. I was surprised to hear it. But now I was shocked. I hadn't heard or thought
of him for years, but three feet from my face I read: "Jack
_____, 8-8-69."

A quarter-century before, a seventeen-year-old Jack had left a
tiny fragment of himself high on the fire tower. Like all the in-

scriptions, it implicitly said: "I'm here. I'm alive in the world." It's a trivial legacy, but that afternoon as I descended my beloved tower flushed with well-being, his graffito was like a motherly slap: Stop! Wait a minute. Consider.

I felt ambushed by coincidence. Or was it simply a matter of focus? Jack's writing probably had—must have—crossed the plane of my vision before, but until I was aware of his dying, I just didn't see it. I stood on the landing and felt bad for him.

But the human ego is ever insistent, ever demanding. Within moments I was factoring Jack's date into my own experience. August 1969 was the summer before my freshman year in college, the month I launched a maiden canoe trip into the Boundary Waters and spotted a bald eagle for the first time.

I checked my journal that evening and realized it was possible that at the time Jack was recording his existence on that strut, I was busily frying hamburgers at the A&W drive-in in our hometown of Chisholm, fifteen miles away. It was a Friday, and conceivably he was in town that night and stopped by for a Teenburger and root beer. I may have seen him and waved. It would've been a forgettable, almost meaningless contact.

But not so that encounter on the fire tower twenty-six years later. I recalled a line of poetry from Sir Walter Scott's *Lady of the Lake* and looked up the passage:

> *Respect was mingled with surprise*
> *And the stern joy which warriors feel*
> *In foeman worthy of their steel.*

Jack's name was a sharp reminder and a challenge. The reminder: I will die—maybe from cancer, maybe on the fireground—but my own tower inscription will also become an epitaph. The challenge: to savor the well-being anyway, to revel in the fact that life is transitory. There is "stern joy" in saying aloud "I could die today," thus banishing self-pity, worry, whining. They are pointless, and a waste of precious, limited energy. If death is the "foeman," it is truly worthy of my steel, because the ever-present potential of death's manifestation catalyzes the life force. So after a brief pause I pounded out another lap, thrilled by the power of my *biceps femoris*.

A year has passed since that autumn afternoon on the fire tower. I've ascended over 450 times. I cannot say that on every single lap I've noted Jack and the exhilaration of my demise. But often, at least, I recognize the pleasing paradox. As my heart drums in my ears with the staccato rhythm of aerobic vigor and I gorge on the vibrancy of forest, lakes, and clouds, I am rushing upward toward death. I hope to make it a good one.

CHAPTER THREE

A Real Fight

How else but in custom and ceremony are
innocence and beauty born?

W. B. Yeats

On a gray afternoon in late December I slip into the fire hall and switch on the lights. Our three trucks—two yellow, one red—burst into radiance, chrome and brass winking in the swelling brightness of the fluorescent bulbs. This illumination of our "fleet" lifts me—it's how I felt as a kid when we plugged in the Christmas tree lights. There isn't a firefighter breathing who doesn't warmly respond to the showy demeanor of a fire engine. Though these vehicles repose silently in their bays most of the time, they project an aura of power and capability—ever primed to transform, surging into vitality with flashing, wailing, and the roaring of raw motive force.

As chief of this rural volunteer fire department, I harbor a special affection, engendered by the mantle of command. Since the buck indeed stops with me, I esteem the promise of those engines as I value the succor of a friend. I usually sigh, though, when I recall how I attained the chief's rank.

On an August evening in 1983, a dozen firefighters were mustered in a quiet circle, leaning against the old '52 pumper or slouched in folding chairs. Most were staring intently at the floor. The chief had just announced his resignation. He'd stay on as a grunt, but he'd had his fill of the top role—needed more time for his family, job, and chores. Someone else would have to carry the ball. No one wanted it. I had been on the department for two years, and though committed, I was still a rookie, nurturing no ambition for promotion.

"Any nominations?" the chief asked. Tense silence. People squirmed, a long minute dragged by. It was embarrassing, and as the pall of indecision settled ever more thickly, pressure mounted for resolution.

I was the first to crack. Against my better judgment, I abruptly volunteered to be the new chief, spontaneously seizing a moment that would change my life. Some might argue, tongue-in-cheek, that such impulsiveness should be sufficient grounds to disqualify a person from being a fire chief. Elevated stress, after all, is endemic to the job description, but I couldn't stand the discomfort of the communal inertia. I was immediately elected by acclamation, garnished with a collective sigh of relief.

Was I qualified? No. Was I enthusiastic? Negative. Was I the best candidate for the position at that time? No way. But there it was: leader by default, because I failed to endure silence and the nervous scraping of feet. I happen to know that many rural chiefs "win" their status via the same or similar means. It's not prudent, but that's how the moment often plays out.

That evening I wielded the leverage I'd just gained, insisting that we amend our bylaws to state that a chief was compelled to serve only two years. I promised that much and no more. It was agreed.

Funny thing is, over a dozen years later I'm still chief. Every other year I call for nominations and/or volunteers, and there are no takers. I forbid the silence to grow oppressive. I raise the issue, survey the assembled membership with a single sweep of eye contact, and proceed to other matters. Why push it? We all know what the floor looks like.

But on this bleak day in late December I'm not in the Fire Hall to reminisce, or even to gaze lovingly at the pretty trucks. My purpose is the performance of ritual.

It's been a bad day, and I'm depressed and lethargic, consumed by self-pity. I know why I'm melancholy, but the mood's foundation is such that nothing practical can be done to alter it. Thus it is pointless to feel lousy all day, and I understand what tonic I require.

I stride to the left rear equipment cabinet on Engine #1 and swing open the doors. A pair of Scott Air-Pak IIA self-contained breathing apparatus(SCBA) hang in their brackets. These are the air tanks and masks you see firefighters wearing on television news reports and in the movies—the devices that make us look so much like Darth Vader that in classrooms nationwide young children are purposely exposed to fire personnel equipped in full turnout gear and SCBAs so if the worst happens, they'll not think that monsters are stalking them in the smoke of a burning building. There have been cases where traumatized kids have resisted rescue—have even hidden—to avoid "Darth Vader."

I automatically check the pressure gauges on each cylinder, then begin the ritual. As in any rite or liturgy, it's important to do it always the same way. I throw on a fire coat, then loosen the buckle that grips the SCBA in its bracket. I swing my right arm through one of the backpack straps of the air tank frame and press it into my shoulder. A gentle tug releases it from the bracket, and I step away, heaving it up onto my back, shoving my left arm through the other strap. I fasten the waist belt and yank it snug, doing the same with the sternum strap and regulator. It rides well enough, tight and stable.

Yea, though I walk through the valley of the
shadow of death, I will fear no evil,
for thou art with me . . .

I feel better already. I am altogether present in the here and now, and the pity and lethargy have receded. I'm focused on something besides myself, concentrating on the utter, life-and-death necessity of knowing that SCBA. Like many firefighters, I'm not completely comfortable in the damn thing—it's heavy, unnatural, and terribly confining. The cylinder contains a limited amount of air, and most people feel slightly claustrophobic while in the grasp (that's what it seems like) of a SCBA. But it is a rescue and survival tool, a way to be temporarily impervious to poisonous smoke (if not claustrophobia), so you have a chance, at least, to save a kid's life.

I pull a Nomex hood over my head and bunch it around my neck. Grasping the black mask of the SCBA in my left hand, I press it against my face. It smells stale and rubbery, and my pulse rate jumps a little, keyed by association of that odor with past terror. There are five tightening straps on the mask—two on each side and one on top. Using both hands, I pull on each side simultaneously, then snug the top. A soft, flexible air hose dangles from the nose cup of the mask. I clutch it and press the open end into my right palm and take a breath. No air. The mask is sealed against my skin. I gather up the Nomex hood and draw it back over my head, flush with the facepiece of the mask. I have no flesh exposed.

Thou preparest a table before me in the presence
of my enemies, thou annointest my head with oil . . .

My blue funk has evaporated. My life and world have regained a broader perspective, and the energy of the moment is zeroed in on technique, proficiency, and the high potential of a trained firefighter armored by a SCBA. I pick up my helmet and thread the air hose through the chin strap, snuggling the suspension onto my head and adjusting it with the knob in back. I jerk the chin strap, make sure the air valve on the regulator is in the "closed" position, then quickly reach down and behind for the main valve on the air cylinder. I twist it open all the way and hear the hiss of pressure at the regulator. I shove the hose into the fitting on the regulator and spin the coupling that secures it, while opening the regulator valve. With my first inhalation, air rushes into the mask, and I hold my breath and listen for leaks around my face. None. I pull on a pair of gloves. I'm ready; I'm "in-service." I am no longer sorry for myself.

> *My cup runneth over, surely goodness and mercy*
> *shall follow me all the days of my life . . .*

I do not cherish the SCBA; I have been too often badly frightened while tangled in its embrace. You don't wear it to picnics. But peering out of the facepiece and hearing my respiration amplified by regulator and mask, I know I have a greater purpose than personal sorrow. And the SCBA reminds me of fear. That's good. Fear transcends self-pity; fear is the wellspring of courage.

A distressing tradition has arisen in some quarters of the fire service, particularly among the vendors and businesses catering to its needs. Firefighters are ceaselessly referred to as "Bravest of the Brave" or "America's Bravest." I see this boast emblazoned on overpriced trinkets ranging from belt buckles to T-shirts. Such dangerous, adolescent bluster makes me acutely uneasy, and you'll never see such a shirt on my back. If anything is repeated often enough (especially via bold commercialization), it eventually waxes insipid and meaningless. But more important, like most people—firefighters included—I regularly doubt my courage. According to the trinkets, I'm supposed to be among "the bravest," but after responding to over 450 fires and other emergencies over the past eighteen years, I don't feel significantly more courageous than when I started. Actually, I feel less so; I'm wiser now, finely attuned to the hazards, sprinkled with tears and blood.

A few weeks after that August evening in 1983 when I became the chief, I described a troubling nervous condition to our family physician. I was jumpy and anxious, perceiving the jitters as a vibrating sensation in my chest and stomach. He offered me a prescription for the symptoms, but suggested the problem was psychological, and interrogated me concerning what stresses I might be supporting in my life. Marital problems? Hassles at work? Death in the family? No, I could lay a finger on nothing specific.

It wasn't until several days later that I was struck by the obvious: it was the newly acquired fire chief position. It seems silly that I didn't suspect that immediately, but the propaganda about the "bravest of the brave," and the pervasive macho drivel that is continually fed to American males, had shielded me from the fact of my natural human vulnerability to strain. I was spooked by being in the chief's boots, sometimes denied sleep by "what if this or what if that?" scenarios spinning through my head. Reality didn't help.

One bitter January night my bedside pager went off at precisely 2 A.M. Pam and I were sound asleep, and the ear-wrenching squawk just happened to coincide with her lurid nightmare. She bolted awake, screaming, and I literally vaulted out of bed to the twin horrors of her bloodcurdling shriek and the ominous, dead-pan delivery of the county dispatcher. I was so startled and un-nerved that it was genuinely painful. My chest constricted, my temples throbbed. I was disoriented, momentarily scared out of my wits. I didn't comprehend a syllable the dispatcher uttered until she automatically repeated the message (somebody's garage ablaze), and then I had to intensely focus to make any sense of it. My hands trembled as I lurched downstairs and pulled on my turnout gear.

The metaphor of firefighters as warriors has been richly developed, and is often valid. Even a volunteer department is in many ways a paramilitary organization. Napoleon Bonaparte, warrior extraordinaire, once offered a keen insight into bravery and command by expressing deep respect for what he termed "two-o-clock-in-the-morning courage," the inglorious demands of emergency in the dead of night, when mind and body are unprepared, fully exposed to the power of terror and confusion—*Phobos* and *Deimos,* the chariot horses of Mars.

As I stumbled out the door into the subzero darkness on that harrowing winter night, I was expected not only to show up, but also to take charge of whatever disaster was unfolding; to ponder (albeit quickly), and to make potentially weighty decisions—knowing that in the first few minutes after the alarm I was fortunate simply to glean the presence of mind necessary to locate my car keys. But I didn't feel brave. I felt responsible; "two-o-clock-in-the-morning courage" is simply the will to duty, prosaic and plodding.

That, of course, is also the essence of my SCBA ritual. It's best to be able to don the Air-Pak quickly, without thinking about buckles, straps, and hose. So once my mask is charged with air, I turn off the air, detach the hose, and shut the cylinder valve. I reverse the initial process and return the unit to its bracket in the cabinet. Then I do it over—faster, cleaner.

> *He restoreth my soul, he leadeth me*
> *in the paths of righteousness . . .*

On our fire hall bulletin board someone has tacked an epigram they clipped out of a fire service journal: "Under stress, you will perform as you train." That is especially critical with a SCBA. I recall one of my first search-and-rescue training sessions. I ended up as humbled as a penitent monk.

Our instructor, provided by a regional technical college, introduced the drill by mentioning that even a few decades ago, firefighters inside a burning building could often, as a last resort, find a breathable atmosphere near the floor. But he assured us that due to the modern proliferation of plastics and the extremely heavy and toxic smoke they emit, if our SCBAs run out of air today, we could easily be "dead meat." He advised us to carry an ax into a structure. If we lost track of the doors and windows, we might be able to hack through a wall—assuming we knew which were outside walls, and assuming they weren't concrete, sheet metal, or something else discouraging. He'd seen a guy do it once—desperate, risky, and definitely inelegant, but it worked—at least for that firefighter that one time. His point was that it's better to avoid trouble in the first place.

"Trouble," of course, is a relative term. As rookies, it seemed to us that simply wearing a SCBA and entering a burning building was pure trouble—never mind running out of air or getting lost. And when the instructor taped paper over our facepieces, my partner Larry and I were initiated into a fresh level of anxiety.

"I want you guys blind," the instructor said. "On most rescue operations you're lucky if you can see your hand in front of your face." A disturbing paradox: while looking for victims we couldn't see anything.

Then he slashed our air supply by two-thirds. Although our tanks are designed to last for thirty minutes, the instructor told us that ten minutes was closer to reality for us. As greenhorns, we would be especially stressed, and our heart rates and air consumption would increase. We would be crawling around burdened by fifty pounds of clothing and gear, caught up in arduous, sustained exertion. A fit veteran might milk a half-hour out of a SCBA, but it was guaranteed we would not. It was foolish, perhaps fatally so, to believe otherwise.

The drill was simple. The instructor set up an obstacle course of boxes and chairs inside our fire hall to simulate the clutter of a residence. One of our fellows would play a semiconscious victim lying somewhere in the "dwelling." He was allowed to groan occasionally, and that would be our sole clue to his location. We would wear our SCBAs, but to spare the cost and inconvenience of refilling cylinders, we didn't actually hook them up. The air hoses were stuffed inside our coats.

Larry and I entered the door of the "burning" building on our hands and knees. I was in the lead, and Larry had his right hand on my left ankle, sweeping his left arm and leg to the outside. We didn't want to miss anyone. I blindly pawed my way along the wall, feeling clumsy and ridiculous. The rest of the department was watching our graceless advance, and I wondered if I looked as unprofessional as I felt. It certainly wasn't like the movies, where fearless firefighters rush through flaming structures like agile half-backs, saving everyone in sight. Apparently they enjoy X-ray vision, are immune to heat, and have no concern for air supply.

Yes, only a drill, but the tension dilated. By the time we turned the first corner—a mere sixteen feet from the door—I was sweating and anxious. We were abreast of a set of shelves, and I was groping among them ("Search everywhere!" the instructor insisted) when we heard the first groan. Larry and I froze. We were like a pair of perked-up hunting dogs, listening for the quarry. Silence.

"It was ahead . . . and to the left," Larry rasped. His voice was distant and weak, muffled by the mask, but I detected an edge to it. That groan had sounded pretty authentic. I didn't think, "Well, our 'victim' is certainly a good actor." Rather, I thought, "What if this was real?" My throat tightened. Behind those taped-over masks we'd meshed with another world, and it was real. This wasn't a training video or a slide presentation. We were in action, searching for a live person, and we were expected to do it right.

I knew we had ten minutes, but my impression of passing time was shattered. The blindness and strain had warped awareness. Had we been crawling for one minute or five? I couldn't guess. Maybe we were almost out of air. A SCBA has a warning bell, and when you hear that dreaded alarm you supposedly have about five minutes of air remaining. But at our accelerated pace of consumption we claimed only ninety seconds. The instructor had a stop watch, and he would call out when we had reached the point of alarm. Then, whether we were saviors or not, we'd have to get out, retracing our route to the door. Theoretically, since we'd already scouted the path on all fours, we could stand up and hurry out like gentlemen. If we couldn't do it in a minute-and-a-half, we were dead.

Larry and I resumed crawling. His grip on my boot was like a vise. We bumped into some "furniture" and searched all around and on top. The cardboard box was about the size of a coffee table, but it seemed to take a full minute to check it. Hurry up! I urged myself. There's someone in here! Imagination convinced me that failure would be disastrous. My body was in metabolic overdrive, fully engaged with the pretend danger and the taut ambience of trial and survival. The rim of my mask was greasy with perspiration. My heart was battering the inside of my eardrums.

We heard another groan. It was still to the left—couldn't be more than ten feet away. We were shuffling alongside two of our fire trucks that served as a "wall." We passed in front of our tanker, my hand on the high bumper. I swept a leg under the truck. Nothing. We scrambled ahead, confident of being close, then ran into the east wall of the building. What was this? I was sure the victim had been within reach.

"Should we keep going around?" Larry suggested. Then another groan—behind us. Confusion was heaped on anxiety. Between us, Larry and I were making a sweep twelve feet wide. How could we miss a prone adult?

We turned back and I grabbed the bumper again. It occurred to me that perhaps the victim was between the trucks, in the "hallway."

"Down this way," I said, excited to have figured it out. But we combed the floor between and under the vehicles and found nothing. Another groan. Behind us again!

"Maybe there's two of them!" I gasped, not really making sense now. We turned to continue through the rest of the building, and the instructor yelled, "Alarm! Alarm! You've got ninety seconds of air!"

It was a drill, right? But for one crazy moment I couldn't breathe. On the verge of panic, I yanked the air hose out of my coat. The inhalation was cool and sweet. Apparently I had pinched the hose shut for an instant. The instructor's shout had been so startling, its import so frightening, that I had locked my arms to my body in a kind of defensive spasm.

Then Larry and I were moving—upright and stumbling for the door. It was a drill, right? But I felt as if I was in a narrow tunnel, closed in, and pursued by waves of flame or a rushing cloud of toxic gas. And we had left someone behind, a groaning human being who would now "die" because of our failure.

We made it to the door in time, but I felt sick. This was a dry run, yet the fear and helplessness were palpable. How would we handle the real thing?

Then the rest of the department burst out laughing. They had been holding back during the drill. Laughing!—because before the exercise the instructor had warned us about psychological denial. When probing a burning building, some firefighters don't want to find anyone. They don't wish to see someone hurt or dead, and do not treasure the terrible responsibility of rescue. He mentioned cases where would-be rescuers had actually brushed against a victim and not realized it. Their minds played tricks, saying, "No, that isn't really a person you've touched, can't be." The subconscious is a bully, and often gets its way. Our fellows were now chuckling because our "victim" had been lying on the bumper of the tanker. Twice—not once, but twice—I'd laid a hand on his foot! And this was a drill. True, the fire-resistant gloves are bulky, but there's a big difference between the textures of steel and flesh. I was mortified.

It wasn't funny to me, but I joined the laughter. It was the nervous, mirthless variety, and I couldn't stop it.

The instructor said he had seen people endure a drill like that and never return—quit the department on the spot. He would shout that they were out of air, and paralysis would strike.

None of us reached that point, but we were deeply impressed. If any had entertained visions of being a dashing, fire-eating hero, an invincible, smoke-snorting Rambo, such fantasies were crushed that evening. We were scared, but it was the brand of fear that builds respect and caution. In the end, ignorance is never bliss, and we had sampled bitter reality.

That watershed session was several years ago, but the taste of smoke and fear remains acrid, so on that gray day in December, I perform the ritual three times—for the Father, the Son, and the Holy Ghost. The SCBA is my monstrance, my chalice. I smile at the notion, but it's a smile of recognition. There are religious overtones to this ritual because the stakes are so high. Some who looked like Darth Vader were closer to Jesus Christ—*and him crucified.*

William James wrote: "If this life be not a real fight, in which something is eternally gained for the universe by success, it is no better than a game of private theatricals from which one may withdraw at will. But it feels like a real fight."

My fire hall ritual works because from inside the mask of an SCBA, I feel as true as the fight.

CHAPTER FOUR

Reaching for Rigel

*The Sea of Tranquillity
rolling on the shores of entropy.
And, beyond,
the intelligence of the stars.*

Stanley Kunitz

I'm a tall white male in America. I have a good vocabulary and graying sideburns. I project an aura of authority and competence. Strangers invariably assume I know what I'm doing. I'm deferred to. I'm a very dangerous individual.

Because, despite my apparent endowments, I'm sometimes incompetent and out of my depth. Since it's usually easy to get my way, and since I often intimidate people (whether I intend it or not), it's also easy to blunder. Not enough people will say to me, "Hey, you're wrong," and stick to it, even when they're right. Given that I'm regularly in charge of hazardous fireground operations, I must always be aware that most people will do as I say, and if I'm wrong, they could be seriously injured or killed.

In mid-August 1994 I was dispatched to a major forest fire in Idaho. The Corral Creek Fire had burned several thousand acres in the Payette National Forest and displayed no inclination to slow down. Sent from Minnesota as a helicopter crew member, I arrived at A-Cabin Helibase on a hectic afternoon as the air operation was burgeoning.

I started on the cargo deck, building sling loads of hose, pumps, rations, tools, and fuel, making sure that the appropriate helicopter was mated with the right load and directed to the proper location. At the peak of the working day, hours passed in a sweaty blur—unloading trucks, loading trucks; spreading cargo nets, rolling cargo nets; slipping swivels into hooks beneath hovering helicopters; scribbling manifests and calculating total payloads; all bracketed by a swig from a canteen and a snack high-graded from an MRE (Meals Ready to Eat). It was fun. It was important, familiar work that I do well. Soon we were keeping seven helicopters flying with cargo, troop shuttles, recon missions, medevacs, and bucket work (water dropping). It was a lively, industrious helibase.

Two weeks into my tour of duty several personnel were rotated out, and a new helibase manager assumed command. He'd been an instructor in a cargo-rappelling class I'd taken in Idaho the previous summer, so to him I was a known quantity in an unfamiliar operation. As we shook hands he said, "You're my new deck coordinator."

I blinked. "But I've never done it."

"That's OK, you'll learn."

A deck coordinator is essentially second-in-command at a helibase; more specifically, the person handles the daily nuts-and-bolts of business: supervising the loadmasters and parking tenders, establishing emergency procedures, overseeing the manifesting and load calculations, helping to design missions, ensuring that people are qualified for their assignments. In a jocular way I've characterized "deck" as a cross between a fire crew boss and an air traffic controller. At a large helibase the job is exhausting—

physically and mentally. In addition to knowing everyone on the base (in this case, about forty people) and their fire and aviation qualifications, it's critical to be aware of the performance and design features of a dozen common models of helicopters, the inner workings of the Incident Command System, and details of the specific fire—general behavior, size, fuels, topography, local weather, water resources, flight hazards (wires, towers, military air routes, etc.), regional fire history, and the location, elevation, and configuration of several helispots.

All this information and more swirls, in an unremitting current, from dawn till dusk. Decisions encompassing everything from the available payload capacity of a Bell 206 Jet Ranger to the siting of a new landing pad to the resolution of a personality conflict are in ceaseless demand. Given the nature of fireground air operations, there's low tolerance for error.

The original deck coordinator was due to return home, and I spent a day and a half shadowing him, watching every move, hanging on every word. I was scared. It was one of the stoutest responsibilities I'd ever been granted. My mood vacillated from *I can do this as well as anyone here* to *I'm definitely in over my head.* I actively practiced stress-reducing tricks. One of the ten Standard Fire Orders is "Stay alert, keep calm, think clearly, act decisively." Yeah, right. Nice sentiment, but how? I once believed you either had the "right stuff" or you didn't. I've changed my mind. Perhaps certain temperaments and personalities are cooler under pressure than others, but keeping calm and thinking clearly are learned skills. My life in fire became more relaxed when I realized that.

The simplest technique has become cliché: take a deep breath. Actually, take two or three deep breaths. As anxiety or panic claw to the surface, pause and inhale; then slowly exhale. It's physiological feedback. When you're breathing steadily, the brain figures things are OK and the panic may be short-circuited.

Another feedback mechanism was summarized by Henry David Thoreau in *Walden*: "What a man thinks of himself . . . determines . . . his fate." I phrase it: if you *act* calm, you will *be* calm; to a surprising degree. For example, a few years ago I was running the second-engine-in to a snappy wildfire that was threatening structures. I knew the initial attack would be complicated and charged with urgency. I knew that I'd be given an important assignment by the incident commander and that I'd be spending a lot of time on the radio. As I approached the scene I took two deep breaths and reminded myself to *speak slowly and clearly* because (1) I needed to be understood, and (2) speaking calmly would project composure to myself and others. A pernicious aspect of fear is that it's highly contagious; panic is an infectious disease. So as the radio chatter began I made a deliberate effort at precise diction and measured cadence. It was a genuine salve. Pretending I was cool helped to make it so. I didn't realize how well the ploy had worked until I returned to the station several hours later. As I rummaged around for a fire report, Fran, our dispatcher, gave me a curious look.

"What?" I asked.

"That fire was a bad one, wasn't it?"

"Yeah, there at the start it was a pretty dynamic situation."

"That's what I thought. Then why did you sound so *bored?*"

I grinned. "Fran, that's the nicest thing you've ever said to me."

That was my goal as the A-Cabin deck coordinator: to exude a calm competence that verged on boredom; to act like a pro, and thus perhaps to be one.

Two days after I assumed the role, the helibase manager had to leave for the afternoon, and he turned the operation over to me. It was a bustling shift and I paced in front of the communications/command tent, monitoring a blizzard of radio traffic. My three assistants juggled eight handheld radios and various log books. Chuck was the take-off-and-landing coordinator, ensuring our immediate airspace was organized and safe. Kathy was the main radio operator, and Harley was the aircraft timekeeper, helping Kathy keep the missions and information straight. I viewed myself and these able people as an isocracy. When in doubt, we worked for consensus, spreading out the authority.

In midafternoon a decision was required about the destination of a large quantity of backhaul, that is, used cargo no longer needed on the line. I thought it should be delivered to point A, and all three of the others thought it should be delivered to point B. I was sure I was right and vigorously built my case, preaching with complete confidence.

Harley was first to be persuaded. Though he was also a tall white male with a good vocabulary, he had less helicopter experience than I, and besides, we were pals—had flown out from Minnesota together. After mulling the options for a moment he said, "OK, I think you're right."

Kathy was next to give in. At first she disputed both Harley and me; but though intelligent, skilled, and assertive, she was also a short female fifteen years my junior. I hammered away until she conceded.

Chuck was another tall white male, about my age, and in the workaday world of the Forest Service would've been my boss—by several levels of management. But he was also quiet and self-effacing and had less helicopter experience. I acted out alpha-male behavior, even standing over them as they sat hunched at a table. Chuck reluctantly agreed to my plan, pressured by three versus one. I had my way. The backhaul ships were routed to point A.

I was wrong. A couple hours later we discovered that Command wanted it at point B.

I apologized profusely to my three colleagues, and allowed myself a lash of shame and terror. The backhaul was not a matter of life-and-death, and my insistence on error produced only inconvenience. But we had to make many decisions that did have potential for serious consequences. I might be sure again. I might convince people of the wrong thing. I might get someone killed.

And thus spooled the stress for the next several days. I embraced a lot of deep breaths, did my share of acting, and denied the tendency to dwell on mistakes.

But besides these techniques, I had another ally: the stars. The elevation at A-Cabin Helibase was over 6,500 feet, and the night sky was majestic, the Milky Way dense and bright, like a sun-drenched cloud. Every evening after dinner, Harley and I and our friend Y. T. strolled down the gravel road toward Goose Lake, admiring the heavens. I pointed out constellations and individual stars, tracing ancient patterns with an eager index finger, offering a running commentary on mythology, astrophysics, and basic navigation. (Y. T. was particularly fascinated, and a couple months later wrote to say that he was exploring the sky with his kids and that "it was a great gift you gave me.") The concerns of the helibase dissolved as I guided them on a journey I'd made myself three decades before.

As a young teen, I was stationed in the backyard, night after night, summer and winter, whenever it was clear. I suspect that no ancient Egyptian or Chaldean priest attempting to decipher the heavens spent more time than I did gazing at the sky. I recognized every constellation in the northern hemisphere, tracing the imaginative patterns of antiquity and following their seasonal trajectories overhead. I knew sixty stars by name, and could recite a few tidbits of information about each—they were acquaintances, my clique.

It was a passion of youth, the unquenchable enthusiasm of innocence. I was fourteen, and my telescope was a small 60mm refractor with a simple altazimuth mount—barely more than a toy—but I watched sunrises on the moon, as the peaks of the Haemus Mountains caught the first rays of lunar dawn from across the Sea of Serenity. I stared at the reddish disk of Mars, hoping for "canals" but happily settling for the polar icecap—tantalizingly glimpsed on an exceptionally transparent night. I tracked the four brightest moons of Jupiter as they orbited the giant planet, performing a slow waltz in my eyepiece. The first time I saw the rings of Saturn—surprisingly distinct and magnificent—I hopped around the yard and yelped, temporarily demented with excitement. I noted the phases of Venus and watched planet Mercury in transit across the surface of the sun. I gaped at the Andromeda galaxy, merely a faint milky oval even in my best eyepiece, but I knew it contained 100 billion suns and was so far away I couldn't conceive of the distance.

But I tried. I tried to understand the universe. I felt kinship with the awestruck ancients—surveying in wonder the same sky and searching for meaning. I saw how easy it would be to regard the stars and planets—migrating nocturnal lights—not as objects, but as oracles. How thin could be the line between astronomer and astrologer.

Five years into this obsession, on July 20, 1969, a pair of American astronauts landed on the moon. As I watched the extraordinary event on television, I was moved to look at the moon, not just an image of it. I had to see if it looked different.

I set up my telescope in the yard. The moon, magnified thirty-seven times through a 20mm Kellner eyepiece, filled the field of view. I focused on Mare Tranquillitatis, the Apollo 11 landing site. I couldn't see the astronauts, of course—hadn't expected to—but I found the moon did look different. Though I'd surveyed the stark lunar features a hundred times and could call dozens of craters, basins, and mountain ranges by name, the moon now appeared even more familiar, more neighborly. It looked less like the moon, and more like American soil—at least during that evening.

Naturally the lunar mission was hailed as one of the greatest adventures of discovery, and it certainly was an astounding enterprise. But consider the voyage of Ferdinand Magellan, who led the first human circumnavigation of the earth. Begun in 1519, the journey was an epoch-making success, the discoveries basic: the theretofore unimagined extent of the Pacific Ocean, the realization that the planet's surface consisted of more water than land (it had long been believed that earth was six-sevenths dry), and, best of all, the knowledge that by means of oceans you could indeed circle the globe.

Today, with our full-color photographs of earth from space, it's difficult to appreciate the magnitude and impact of Magellan's discoveries. Whole systems of geography, and even a few cosmological and theological dogmas, were proved wrong. For those who still believed the earth was flat, an entire worldview fell by the wayside. As stupendous as it was, the Apollo 11 mission could not have such effect.

This experience of discovery—of seeing the world from a new perspective—is not something limited to a fortunate few. We can all launch our own missions of exploration. A year or so after I started searching the sky, I made a notable discovery on a cold, clear night in February. It was the first time I seriously tried to comprehend the distance to the stars.

I was familiar with the term "light-year"—the distance traveled by a beam of light in one year's time at a velocity of 186,000 miles per second—and that night I attempted to understand exactly what that meant. I was young, of course, and in a restless, questing mood. I stood gazing at Rigel, the bright bluish star in Orion's leg, transfixed by the notion that Rigel is 750 light-years away.

I recalled a thought experiment I'd inadvertently conducted as a young child. I had a set of Lincoln Logs, a toy that absorbed me for hours on end as I built model log structures of various designs. One winter evening I completed a cabin of which I was particularly fond. I folded a white sheet of paper over the roof to simulate snow, then placed a small flashlight inside and turned out the lamp in my room. I gazed at the warm little house with delight and longing. I wanted to be in that cabin. I imagined it. Then: What if I had a tiny set of Lincoln Logs inside there and built another cabin inside the first? Then an even smaller—microscopic—boy would be inside that house to construct yet another replica, tinier still, and so on and so on until my mind reeled. I remember thinking I'd stumbled upon a strange new idea, and I pondered *infinity*—though I didn't hear the word until years later.

On that February night I employed a similar technique to grasp the distance to Rigel. I projected my vision toward the star. What if the backyard were as large as the earth, and earth were as large as the sun, and the sun as big as the solar system, and the solar system as wide as the distance to the nearest star? I lost track of time.

Suddenly my concentration broke. Stunned, I realized I couldn't comprehend a light-year. The world exploded in my face. The normal, mind-assuaging lines of perspective skewed, and I was overwhelmed by the immensity of the universe. With a flash of insight I understood the sky was not up: it was all around me. I wasn't looking up at the stars, but out at the stars from the surface of a tiny sphere. For the first time I was aware of being on a planet, a literal spaceship, and the stars were outside, surrounding it. There were stars "under" the earth too, under my feet. I was an astronaut.

I became cognizant of the earth gently curving away toward South America. I turned and sensed earth sloping for the North Pole. The sky was resolved into an incredibly deep, three-dimensional galaxy-shape. I was enveloped in it. I focused on Polaris, the target of earth's axis, and for a precipitous few moments I was falling toward the North Star. I gasped and quickly shifted my attention to our old lopsided garage. Gravitational pull returned in a rush and I regained the familiar rooted sensation of a planet-dweller. But the stars have never been the same.

Magellan's circumnavigation and Apollo 11's landing made history. But to me they are not more significant than what I discovered by staring at Rigel from my own backyard. My fleeting altered state spurred me to further study. Just how big was the universe? I pulled three books from the local library shelves and found three different estimates for the distance to the Andromeda Galaxy, ranging from 1.5 to 2.2 million light-years, and to this day it's probable that none of them is correct. In short, nobody really knows how far it is to Andromeda, or just how big the universe might be.

As an amateur astronomer I found that comforting. Our precocious species still isn't certain about something as basic as the size of our "neighborhood," to say nothing of its origin, age, or exact composition. Good. There is still mystery—even after millennia spent peering at the sky, and the last three and a half centuries with telescopes. That made nights spent in the backyard all the more alluring. I was traversing little-known territory, a celestial wilderness. The sky was still a realm of surprise and suspense. It was unlikely I would add to humanity's store of astrophysical knowledge (though there was always the chance of spotting a nova or a new comet), but I was seeing the cosmos for myself—gleaning raw, unfiltered data. Firsthand, under clear, chilly skies I could wonder, why is it so big? If you had a spacecraft that clipped along at 100,000 miles per hour, it would take over 26,000 years to reach Proxima Centauri, the nearest star (about four light-years away). Why arc things so spread out?

I considered three possibilities:

1. The incomprehensible vastness of the universe was meant to elicit our collective metaphysical gasp. The power or being responsible for the cosmos wanted us to be very impressed.

2. Such distances provided a mighty, eons-lasting challenge, perhaps one we could never meet, and hence we would always have something to strive for—the stars.

3. The various galactic civilizations, each a unique experiment, needed to be utterly isolated.

This last was at the core of my devotion to starlight. Was there extraterrestrial life—other intelligent races—studying other skies and wondering if we were out there somewhere? I had no evidence, of course, but I believed it with all my heart. Did those multitudes of stars and galaxies exist only to serve as beguiling sparkles in the night sky of planet earth? That seemed highly implausible.

My fantasy was that one night I would see a UFO up close and convincing, and the occupants would offer some token of their reality. Perhaps they'd take me for a ride. A long ride. Because I didn't want to just look at the moon, I wanted to land there. I wanted to trek on the Martian deserts and orbit Jupiter while perched on a crater rim of Ganymede. I wanted to weave through the rings of Saturn and skip across the cloud tops of Venus. I wanted to spend the night on some distant planet where the Andromeda galaxy filled half the sky. I loved to gaze at the stars, but only because I wanted to go to the stars.

But those distances—would any species ever learn to master them? Devise a means to journey from star to star in weeks or months instead of millennia? I hunched over my telescope, an instrument only marginally better than the one Galileo used in 1609, and willed it to happen—wished and dreamed that it would. I was a votary of celestial faith and romance. I was a disciple of science fiction and the "space age." And like any pious believer of ages past, I longed to go to heaven.

And so I do. I call it astronomical happiness. It's joy in the presence of beauty; awe in the presence of sheer magnitude; wonder at cosmic enigmas. But most of all it's a passage beyond the self. The warrior's passage.

We are needy, self-absorbed, biological creatures whose fundamental instinct is for survival and propagation. Any time we can transcend the tyranny of our genes is a precious time. For me, the night sky is a portal to transcendence. Temporary, of course; relatively brief spans of selflessness are the best that flesh and blood can manage. To me the stars say, get real; notice the scope of the universe. Your own concerns are not trivial, but assign them a cosmic perspective—at least for a little while. It's a blessed privilege in our terrestrial barracoon to be friends with the stars, capable of plumbing the celestial matrix and saying, Wow.

So each night at A-Cabin Helibase the anxieties of the day would be vaporized by the light from a myriad of distant suns. A deep breath was redundant; it would only be snatched away.

And in the frosty mornings before dawn, when I rolled out of my sleeping bag to engage a new day, the southeast sky was spangled by Orion and Rigel. Old comrades. Brave companions. A tonic.

CHAPTER FIVE

Thirty Pounds

*For another, better thing than a fight
required of duty exists not for a warrior.*

Bhagavad Gita

A column of smoke is like a crystal ball. Properly construed, it reveals your future. The color, density, size, and drift forebodes what's burning and how enthusiastically, long before firefighters arrive on the scene.

That's why my expectations shifted into a higher gear when I glimpsed the smoke from the Duckling Fire. The column was viscid, burgeoning, and pitch black. It had been reported as "a fire in the woods" by the citizen who dialed 911, but that seemed wrong. Not only was the forest soggy, but such wicked smoke was more characteristic of burning petrochemicals: asphalt shingles, plastic pipes, curtains, clothing.

The dispatcher could offer only a general location—a stretch of gravel back road—so when I noted the ominous brand of smoke, I steered for the sole residential address in that area, suspecting ugliness.

I swung into the driveway and realized the citizen caller had been partially correct. A patch of woods was indeed burning, and a brace of midsized Norway pines torched out at that moment, ignited by the horrific radiant heat of a small house totally invested in flame.

I parked my pickup on the shoulder, a hundred yards back and out of the way. As I threw open the door I heard an explosion. I assumed it was a fuel tank of some kind, probably propane. On my handheld radio I also noted one of our engines reporting an "enroute" to dispatch. I hailed them and outlined the situation.

"Bring everything," I said.

As I hustled toward the inferno on foot, sorting out the visual farrago of the fireground, and reminding myself—aloud—to stay calm, I encountered two civilians. One was the distraught homeowner, a man in his twenties. He was clutching a cardboard box filled with a dozen cheeping ducklings.

"Is everyone out of the house?" I asked.

He nodded and lifted the box.

"Good. Get clear of this area."

I made three brisk judgments that would shape our initial attack: the house was a total loss; the wildfire was anemic and spreading slowly; our main problem was a hundred-pound propane cylinder several feet from the structure. Heat impingement had triggered the vessel's pressure relief valve, and the escaping gas had ignited. It was shooting blue flame like a blowtorch. That was "normal," but enough heat could still cause the cylinder to rupture with catastrophic force—a fuel-air bomb. The flame had already touched off some piled lumber, applying additional heat to the cylinder. Our first mission was to cool that tank. I didn't covet another explosion.

A floatplane roared overhead, skirting the smoke. It was a Minnesota Department of Natural Resources (DNR) Beaver that I'd heard on the radio. The pilot had spotted the column and altered course for a recon. As he banked away he reported to his DNR contact that he intended to land on Big Sturgeon Lake, rig his aircraft for water drops, and commence bombing the fire.

I switched my radio to his frequency.

"That's a negative, Jim," I snapped. "No water drops, I repeat no water drops. I have a propane cylinder involved and your aircraft will be a distraction."

"Copy that."

I hoped this spurned offer of assistance didn't sound too harsh, but I didn't dwell on it. Interagency public relations could wait.

Engine #1 pulled in front of my pickup, and two firefighters scrambled out of the cab. Another of our people had just arrived in his own car. Engine #2, our pumper/tanker, was a minute or so away. By now I had a litany of commands on the tip of my tongue.

"Steve and Tom, deploy both preconnects. One to the back of the house for the wildfire, and one this way"—pointing—"to cool a propane cylinder. Thor, cover the propane tank. When #2 gets here we'll use the guy's duck pond"—I'd seen it west of the house— "for a water supply."

Thor, a rookie, grabbed the nozzle of one of our 150-foot, inch-and-three-quarter preconnected hoses (so-called because they're already threaded to a pump outlet), and I helped him advance it toward the cylinder. Even from fifty feet we could feel heat from the house—like the open door of an oven. We crouched low into cooler air, and I clamped a hand to Thor's left shoulder. He could see the blue blowtorch for himself.

"Lay a stream on it," I said. "Hit the top and let water flow down the sides."

He nodded and I called out to Steve at the engine pump controls. "Hit it!"

The hose filled, contracting into shallow curves like a sunbathing snake. Thor cracked open the nozzle and air hissed out ahead of the water. I grabbed the line behind his arm, and as water burst from the nozzle it kicked like a shotgun. Finally. We were shooting, we were attacking. It was only a few minutes since I arrived, but time limps before you get water. I drew a deep breath; I'd been inadvertently holding it.

I motioned for another firefighter to replace me on the line, then rushed over to help Tom with the second preconnect.

"Stay back for now," I said. "Just hit the edge of the grass and brush until that propane tank is stabilized."

Three more firefighters were there with Engine #2, and I directed them to start laying a three-inch supply line to the duck pond.

"We'll set up the floating pump and hook to #2. Refill #1 and keep it in reserve. No hose streams on the house for now, it's a loser." Until we established a water supply it was wasteful to spew precious liquid on a structure that was now collapsing onto its foundation.

Within ten or twelve minutes of the call we had eleven firefighters and all three engines on scene, and for the next two hours we sprayed and pumped, hosed and humped, heaved and chopped, shouted and laughed, battled and sweat. We did not—could not—save the house, but we neutralized the propane cylinder/bomb, snuffed the wildfire, protected an outbuilding, and toiled as a team—an elated band of brethren. Nobody got hurt. After the initial fear, and before the last grubby struggles of mop-up, it was pulse-pounding fun. It was service and duty, honorable and esteemed. Despite his loss of almost everything, the homeowner gushed in gratitude to see so many of his neighbors speed to his aid as volunteers.

It was a good operation (some are not), but by the end I was on my knees as we pulled several hundred feet of dirty wet hose back to the trucks. A few days before I'd injured my back, and despite a brace, the pain was occasionally too intense for upright posture. When my buddies asked what happened, I flashed a crooked smile. It was a fire injury. I'd been teaching a wildland fire suppression class, and at one point had to shift a small lectern that was blocking a projection screen. I half-lifted, half-dragged it for a total of three feet, then felt a sickening dagger of pain in my lower back. It would require fifteen days of care and cautious stretching for the hurt to abate.

But as I knelt in the muddy yard and eased out of my soaked fire coat, I appreciated the pain as part of the transition from the éclat of the fireground back to daily habits—from the luster of earnest combat to the flatness of obligatory habit. A sore back is cliché. Much of life is shaded by necessary mediocrity. I was easing down to that. Most of us soar through existence in spurts; we are usually pedestrians.

Next day, I hung my wet turnout gear on the clothesline and returned to the garden—on my knees—where I'd been weeding the asparagus bed when the pager sounded for the Duckling Fire. Still coming down, level with the dandelions now and meeting an occasional earthworm while swatting mosquitoes.

With dirt under my fingernails I filled out a fire report that afternoon, then took a red zippered duffel bag to the clothesline. My gear was dry. I removed wadded newspaper from inside my steel-toed rubber boots and shoved them into the legs of my bunker pants. I rolled the pants down over the boot tops and arranged the suspenders so they wouldn't tangle. I now could just step into the boots and yank the pants to my waist. I laid them in the bottom of the bag. I unpinned my coat and stuffed the pockets with fire gloves, a spanner, a flashlight, and a Nomex hood. I folded the coat and packed it next to the pants. I wiped the faceshield of my helmet and tucked it inside. I zippered the bag shut and carried it to the back porch. I laid my radio and an extra battery on top. Ready.

An hour or so later I headed to the store for a gallon of milk, and on the way out the door I hefted the gear bag. It weighs thirty pounds. Not terribly heavy, but certainly more ponderous and inconvenient than a set of keys, a checkbook, or most anything else I regularly portage out to the truck. With a twinge of pain in my back I hauled the thirty pounds to the garage and hoisted it into the box of the pickup. I do this every single time I leave the house. As a volunteer I'm on call 24 hours a day, 365 days a year (unless I'm out of town). I try hard never to be separated from my gear. It's in the house or it's in the truck. Ready. Always.

As I drove to the store, passing the intersection where I'd turned to race to the fire the day before, it occurred to me that this daily routine is the meat of my fire-fighting vocation. Towering flames and exploding fuel tanks are the exception—in this rural area, almost an aberration. Lugging my thirty-pound gear bag from the house to the truck, from the truck to the house, time after time, day after day, year after year is the nut of accountability. Carrying your gear. That is the deep batholith of duty, the well-spring of performance. It's simple to show up at a fire. It's natural to be aroused by emergency and addicted to adrenaline. That thirty pounds is a burden. That bulky bag is an omnipresent pain in the ass. A drag.

But it's also the crux, the pivot dividing the professionals from the dilettantes. Carrying your gear is the core of virtue. You just carry your gear.

CHAPTER SIX

An Evening at the Triangle

Glory is like a circle in the water.

William Shakespeare

My boss and I sauntered away from the helicopter pad, Forest Service fire packs slung over our shoulders and flight helmets cradled in our arms. I joked that it was the high point of the mission—we were lions, cool and photogenic, backlit by a westering Idaho sun.

"Yeah," he added, deadpan, "just like a beer commercial."

We laughed happily, a touch giddy after our first wildfire dispatch of a wet, tedious season. We hadn't even reached the fire—a smoky, half-acre spot near Lightning Creek. We were enroute when the incident commander (IC) requested that we land at a grass airstrip in the vicinity and "stand by." He had an engine crew approaching the blaze via logging road, and had also ordered smoke jumpers. Shortly after we landed, eight of them parachuted to the fire, and a few minutes later the IC radioed that helicopter support was unnecessary.

Our pilot cracked a lopsided smile. When the dispatch had come in, he was packed and ready to leave on a weekend trip to Spokane, and we had kidded him earlier in the day that such well-laid plans were bound to be upset. Besides, he'd spent a year piloting helicopters for the Green Berets in Vietnam and had flown a lot of fire missions since; he relished action, and we'd had none for the past month. On our way to the fire he keyed the intercom and quipped, "This flying thing is kinda fun—be nice to do more of it."

Still, my boss and I were cheerful. At least we'd almost made it to a fire, and had tallied two hours of overtime to boot. Only generous overtime made it financially expedient for me to be 1,400 miles from Northeastern Minnesota in the summer, paying rent and missing home. After nearly four weeks in the Nez Perce National Forest, these were the first hours of OT—not a good omen.

One source of consolation and camaraderie for underpaid and sometimes homesick firefighters is the Triangle Tavern in Grangeville, Idaho. The Triangle, or more jocularly, "the T-Club," derives its name from the wedge-shaped "corner" it occupies, formed by the angular intersection of North D and Pine Streets, near the grain elevators and railroad tracks at the north edge of town. The single, smoked window faces the forested flanks of Blacktail Ridge, and the door—usually ajar in the summer swelter—opens to the undulating grain and grass fields of the Camas Prairie.

To categorize the Triangle as a blue-collar or "workingman's" bar is a hopeless understatement. In July and August, just three vocations are represented in the ramshackle, wonderfully decrepit little saloon—lumbering, farming, and wildland firefighting. The price of tap beer is fifty cents—almost a formality—and everyone's a hero. Rounds for the house are as ubiquitous as laughter, and on many T-Club forays I'd quaffed free beer all evening while fruitlessly shouting for the privilege of treating the house myself. The competition to buy for buddies (and strangers) is fierce, and the down-home warmth of the Triangle transforms newcomers into "family" in hours, or even minutes.

One night a couple of summers ago, a tourist from Alaska wandered in by chance (the establishment is not mentioned by AAA or any other tourist bureaus, public or private) and was so taken with the ambience and fellowship that he hurried out to his Winnebago and returned with several smoked salmon, which were duly passed around the bar. By the end of the evening he was as "local" as anyone, and vowed to return.

The joint is no roomier than a rich man's den, so when the seats are taken it's OK to perch on the pool table, sit astride empty kegs (usually in ample supply), or spill out into the street and lounge on the tailgates of dusty pickups that smell of saw gas and bar oil.

After our abortive but welcome dispatch—a portent, I hoped, of OT to come—I hiked to the Triangle for some celebratory beer. I'd had the good sense to rent a room within walking (or stumbling) distance. A half-dozen smoke jumpers were already deployed at the bar, toasting the Nez Perce Forest's first fire jump of the season.

Smoke jumpers are generally considered the national elite of the wildfire corps—by both themselves and the rest of us. (A few years ago they were featured in a documentary film entitled *Wilderness Warriors*.) As with most generalizations, it's not completely accurate. Some members of the jumper aristocracy are excellent firefighters, some are not; what's universally admired is the high grade of skill, confidence, and teamwork required to safely parachute into forested mountain terrain—before even engaging the fire itself. Considering the inherent dangers, the US Forest Service and Bureau of Land Management smoke jumper organizations can be justly proud of how few jumpers have been killed or crippled in the past fifty-plus years, and how effective they've often been on the fireground. It's one thing to make a parachute jump at an airport or other expansive commercial drop zone—

many thousands of people (myself included) have done it—but it's playing in an entirely different league to ride a canopy into a small open spot in the mountains, avoiding tall timber, snags, and rocks, or sometimes landing in or on same. Then, in a fever of exertion, you metamorphose into a fire grunt, realizing that when the fire is extinguished you may have to pack your jump and fire gear (perhaps a hundred pounds or more) for several rugged miles out to the nearest road or helispot.

Most smoke jumpers, I think, can be forgiven if they display satisfaction in their station and tend to emphasize the exclusive nature of their small club. (In 1996 there were about 360 active jumpers in the US.) Self-esteem and *esprit de corps* are important factors in maintaining the morale and integrity of outfits that are regularly exposed to high potential hazard. As a member of a helitack crew—also a dangerous role at times (in fact, more helicopter people have been killed than jumpers)—I fully appreciate the value of pride and unit cohesiveness, but I also realize we are not as glamorous as smoke jumpers. Such is their storied fame that when I migrate to the West for the summer fire season, many of my acquaintances assume that I'm a smoke jumper. When I explain that no, I work with helicopters, and I outline the details of my job, eyes glaze over. A half-century of sometimes florid publicity has ensured that the general public grasps the parachute/forest-fire blend, but "helitack" remains arcane.

After my first season in Idaho, a close friend asked me, "Just what is it you do out there?" I launched into a long and colorful account of wildfire initial attacks, search and rescue missions, fire recon (both visual and infrared), medevacs, and the support and supply of smoke jumpers. He appeared to listen attentively, but the next year he mailed a package of goodies and enclosed a note: "Share this with your fellow jumpers." I sighed and did as instructed.

After three seasons in the Nez, I was more or less accepted by the jumpers—not as an equal, certainly, but as an associate, a fellow firefighter and member of the air operations team. Most of the jumpers seemed to feel that though the helitack crew wasn't as excellent as they, we might be better than most. But because we often "sligout" their jumpgear (sparing them long pack-outs), some jumpers tend to view the helicopter crew as their personal servants. I remember well my first day at the base. I introduced myself to one of the jumpers and she replied, "So. You're the new heli-slug?" If there was a more succinct method of delineating my relative status, I never encountered it.

On this summer night, I had barely ducked through the narrow portal of the T-Club when a frosty glass of Olympia draft was thrust into my hand, courtesy of one of the smoke jumper squad leaders. He was brimming with beer and bullshit, crowing about the fire jump. Two hours before he had ripped the ball cap off his head and flung it at me in a display of mock disgust as I donned my flight and fire gear. Our helicopter had been dispatched first, and it seemed to be our show. The cap-throwing highlighted an undercurrent. I knew that the feigned anger and good-natured contempt ("What the hell is this!? They're calling for damn rotorheads!") was centered on a gritty core of snobbery and scorn.

I grasped the free beer, chugging it for a quick rush of refreshment, and another appeared almost instantly. The smoke jumpers were in excellent humor. I leaned against the jukebox and sipped the second brew, listening to the banter.

They were loudly dissecting the minutiae of the fire jump, from the dispatcher's call to the flight home. In drier, more brazen seasons, it would've been an utterly routine operation, unworthy of long-winded analysis, but this was the first gig of a slow year, and we'd all been pining for fresh stories. One virtue of the jump was that it paid off a lucrative kitty. A calendar running from early July to mid-August had been pinned up in the ready room, and for five bucks you purchased a day, predicting the date of the first fire jump. Memories and records of hotter seasons were canvassed, and soon the pot was worth $115. A groan of collective envy echoed through the base when it was realized that the winner of the kitty had also jumped the fire, and was thus cashing in on the OT and the glory as well as the wager. An investment tip for his windfall was quickly scribbled beside his name on the ready-room board: "$115 divided by 50 cents = 230 beers at the T-Club. Pay up!" Since he and his comrades were spending the night on the fireground, the actual balancing of that equation would have to wait.

The squad leader who'd served as spotter for the mission, that is, selected the jump site and told people when to exit the aircraft (called a "jump master" in sport parachuting), was saying that the fire "was really only a 'four-manner.' " Everyone nodded, acknowledging that between eight jumpers and an engine crew, it was a clear case of initial attack overkill.

"What the hell," someone chimed in, "just call it training."

Heads bobbed again. Given the anemic nature of the season it was not unreasonable to seize any opportunity for action. Nothing dulls the fine edge of a fire crew more than inactivity, and no one anticipated any administrative flak because of overstaffing a fire at this stage of the game.

That caused everyone to remember the helitack crew—might just as well have sent us in too. But I guess the IC figured that would be pushing it.

The squad leader flashed me a cockeyed grin and said that even though they'd been dispatched to the fire, it was an anxious flight. Would they be turned around before they arrived? With an engine crew enroute and our helicopter already in the air, he fully expected a dry run. Then he heard the IC tell us to land and stand by. His grin widened, and he reenacted the scene in the jump plane: "I said 'All right!' and gave a 'thumbs-up' to Walt," he jerked up this thumb—Walt was on a nearby stool, "because I knew then that the fire was ours and you guys were screwed!"

He was maliciously gleeful all over again, just as he must've been in the aircraft. But suddenly he looked away, sheepishly red-cheeked and obviously embarrassed by such a prideful admission.

It was a curious moment, fraught with that complex affliction—honesty.

He had sincerely wished to rub it in that the jumpers were utilized and we weren't—gloating is a cheap way to enhance your advantage, and we all knew this puny fire cried out for enhancement. But a part of his firefighter's psyche, usually displayed on our sleeves as prominently as a shoulder patch, instantly conceded that gloating (especially in such a small matter), was unprofessional—was in fact utterly "bush league," a relic of the grade-school playground.

Perhaps the beer had loosened the squad leader's tongue, but nevertheless, I'd glimpsed his true colors. There was a core of arrogance (no great revelation) fueled by a genuine vein of insecurity (that startled me a little), and I was the straw man knocked down for the sake of his self-esteem.

I retaliated by rendering myself even more vulnerable. It was a gamble, but I said, "Hey! What's the deal? I was happy when I heard you guys get dispatched—a little action for everybody. I thought we were a team." I sounded offended, and I was.

His fellow jumpers were listening, and I held my breath. Here's where they could hammer me, the pivotal moment when such heli-slug pretension could be nailed to the wall: *Team? What the hell do you mean? Heli-slugs in the same huddle as jumpers? Who recruited you?* But they didn't.

The squad leader tried another grin that was even more crooked and sheepish, and mumbled an acknowledgment into his beer.

I had him then, could really have unleashed a zinger, like actually verbalizing "bush league." But I realized that such a cutting remark in that context would itself be unprofessional. The squad leader's embarrassment was as potent as his pride, and I was touched by his insecurity. Here was a skilled, experienced firefighter and smoke jumper, with a leadership role in an elite and celebrated organization, and a part of him felt compelled to put me down—

someone who was in no way a threat to his position and status in the fire service hierarchy, a heli-slug.

It was fear, of course, and I admit to a wicked gratification that the squad leader revealed it so blatantly. We're all afraid at times, and it's reassuring to see it confirmed that someone whose skill you admire also knows fear. I'm not referring to a dread of death or injury. We all think about that, naturally, but not much; there's no point. Rather, it's as British Colonel Haking said over ninety years ago: "The British officer has sometimes failed in war because he was afraid, not of the enemy or of being shot, but of doing the wrong thing."

The colonel could well have been speaking of firefighters, and especially of those involved in critical air operations—such as smoke jumping and helitack—where mistakes can be obvious, and sometimes newsworthy, and where the margin for error is almost always narrow. Getting hurt is ugly, but causing someone else to suffer injury is horrible, contemptible.

I was also gratified to note that when I mentioned the team, a couple of jumpers nodded. We were. And yes, it was partially the beer talking when the squad leader rubbed in our helitack crew's misfortune that afternoon, but beer (and banter) can also lubricate *esprit de corps,* and the squad leader bought me a third one—to atone, I think, for his outburst. He had done a wrong thing. Later, he and I fell into a debate on some tactical matters, and politely heard each other out, arguing as colleagues.

Like any association of humans, the fire service doesn't always live up to its ideals—there's political maneuvering, favoritism, posturing, venality. But in my experience, the service is still more of a genuine meritocracy than not, and in that system, especially in light of the paramilitary nature of firefighting, a hierarchy is essential. Not only a formal chain of command, but a natural stratification of the adequate, the good, the best.

"A society without an aristocracy," wrote Ortega y Gasset, "without an elite minority, is not a society." That holds true, at least, for the fire service.

It's good that smoke jumpers are proud, consider themselves special. An honest elite can draw others upward, serving as an uncontested measuring rod. It's OK for a smoke jumper squad leader to believe he's a better firefighter than I—whether it's true or not—so long as he also believes that at some more basic level we are equals; as long as we can share the stools (or the kegs) at the Triangle Tavern and argue long into the night, fighting tenaciously for the privilege of buying the next round.

CHAPTER SEVEN

The Best of Mistakes

The strongest of all warriors are these two—
Time and Patience.

Leo Tolstoy

For most, life is only rarely as dramatic as a parachute jump or a helicopter flight to a fire. But everyday challenges, often surging from our own emotional centers, are usually more difficult to master. One of my chronic, mundane struggles was exposed by the lure of an esoteric board game.

During a blustery silver dusk in November 1995, I skated with friends on the lake outside their back door. A sheet of fresh snow unfurled the illusion of gliding across an ivory plain. Heads down and arms pumping, we skated for a half-mile against a stiff west wind, then turned and sprinted east down the ice—sometimes just standing straight up, blades together, arms raised to snag the force of the zephyr.

Back near shore we batted a tennis ball with hockey sticks, playing keep-away from their quick and zealous golden retriever. It was invigorating fun, accented by the knowledge that it was short-lived. Inevitably, more snowfall would render the lake unskatable.

Indoors after dark, we warmed ourselves with hot chocolate, and in the midst of an anecdote Catherine mentioned "the Go club."

I interrupted. "What's a Go club?" It was a casual inquiry, a conversational lubricant.

"You're not familiar with Go?"

Her demeanor became animated. I sensed I'd broached a big topic, and some revelation was at hand. Little did I realize that metaphorically, I was like the Spanish explorer López de Cárdenas, the first white man to stumble upon—in astonishment—the Grand Canyon. My amazement would come later, but Catherine aroused my curiosity.

She explained that Go is an ancient Chinese board game roughly similar to chess, though more complicated. When she lived in the Twin Cities she was the only female player at a club devoted to Go.

"I'll show you," she said, and briskly left the room. Her partner, Chris, sported a bemused grin.

"Brace yourself," he said. "But I think you'll be intrigued."

Catherine returned with a wooden board divided into 361 squares, 19 by 19 (compared to 64 squares, 8 by 8 for chess), and a box of glass "stones," 180 coin-sized white ovals and 181 black. Clinching a stone between her index finger and thumb, she snapped it onto the board with a ringing echo of glass on wood. Unlike in chess, the pieces are played on the intersections of the lines forming the squares, not in the squares themselves. Once played, they cannot move. The object of the game is to employ your stones to surround and hold more territory—the points of intersection—than your opponent. The basic rules of play are so simple they can be mastered in a few minutes by children. But the astronomical number of permutations generated by the elementary "initial conditions" is mind-boggling. One of the many books about the game states that "the number of possible combinations of moves is said to exceed the number of subatomic particles in the universe."

As she outlined the rules and placed stones on the board, Catherine talked about "making shapes" and the sometimes intuitive rather than calculated nature of tactics and strategy. Computers programmed to play Go can still be routinely beaten by even midlevel human players. I reached into the box, and the smooth stones were pleasant to fondle—first cool, then warm to the touch. Catherine mentioned a few words of Go language, poetic and captivating Asian terminology like *atari*, similar to "check" in chess (and yes, the source of the electronic game manufacturer's name), or the mysterious *sente*, a word describing the flow of initiative between players during a game, the precise meaning of which is still being debated after centuries of usage. A rough synonym *might* be "momentum," depending on the warp and woof of a particular match. I found the jargon seductive, and was astounded when Catherine produced a book that preserved, move-by-move, various famous games played between Japanese masters in the shogun's palace two and three centuries ago. Some aspects of these contests are still being hashed over by current Go aficionados, dissected with the fervor usually reserved for historical events. Chris was right, I was intrigued. But I had to leave.

"I'll have to try this sometime," I said cheerily, as I might mention my desire to sample a flavor of pie, or pick up a magazine—in other words, without proper respect. Catherine shot me a skeptical glance that in retrospect I realize meant: many are called but few are chosen.

She loaned me an article about Go that she'd written for a newspaper several years before. It included diagrams of basic moves, and I read it the next day. I was still interested, but daily concerns and sundry deadlines intruded, and I forgot about it for two weeks.

Then my wife, Pam, spotted an ad in a magazine for a beginner's book about Go that came with a cheap paper board and set of paper "stones." The ad copy stated that a Go set would be aboard the next Space Shuttle flight and that President Clinton was being urged to learn "the ultimate game." I bought it, literally.

A few days later Pam and I traded the book back and forth, reading the first five chapters, then played our initial halting game. We quickly discovered that the level of concentration required was almost hypnotic. It seems impossible to play Go without becoming utterly absorbed. At the end we were startled to note that an hour and a half had passed without reckoning. I was hooked.

And amazed. For the first time in my life I began systematically studying the tactics and strategy of a board game—drilling daily with the stones, working through scenarios and games outlined in the manual. Every morning my written task list included "Go practice," enshrined with such basic missions as "haul in firewood" and "change oil in truck."

I borrowed that book of famous shogun's palace games from Catherine and spent several winter evenings at the kitchen table, painstakingly reconstructing the masterful contests. I would spend up to two hours laying stones on the board, only partially comprehending what I was seeing and doing. One game—called "Dosaku's Masterpiece" and played on November 19, 1683—encompassed 277 moves, and after 86 moves I was humbled and awed to read in the commentary accompanying the diagrams: "Black 86 was another good move. At this stage both players probably knew Shunchi was going to win by one point." Say what? How? It was like reading the liturgy for an initiation into some mysterious and arcane rite.

I decided that Go seduced via three fundamental attractions: the beauty of the board, stones, and patterns; the alluring antiquity of the game; and most important, its difficulty—especially for me. My aptitude for structural visualization and analyzing complicated patterns is weak. The functions of mechanical arrangements obvious to others often baffle me. Where Pam instantly sees connection and figuration, I see chaos. And indeed, she quickly gained the upper hand in our first few games. Only through practice and intense study (I read our introductory manual three times) did I finally manage to overcome her innate knack for deciphering the protean complexity of the board.

Practicing Go became a discipline—like working out or meditating—and I made rapid progress, or so I imagined. After three weeks of immersion in the game I played Catherine at a Christmas gathering. She gave me a nine-stone handicap; that is, I placed nine stones on the board at prescribed strategic locations known as *star points* before she was allowed her first play. That afforded me a colossal advantage. Her position was akin to a chess player beginning a game with no pawns and being placed in check by an opponent's first move.

She crushed me. And did so while following two conversations and munching snacks. I certainly hadn't expected to win, but the scale of my defeat was stunning. Long hours of study had barely nicked the vast diamond surface of Go's potential. I realized the game was so deeply stratified that I understood almost nothing.

I vigorously returned to the drills and gradually began to peel back the veils. That's what it seemed like: each time I played a game the board appeared in a fresh light. There were several "ah ha!" moments as elaborate patterns of stones suddenly made sense in the broader aspect of a game. I likened it to my decades-long theological study, when I believed that the profound symbolism of Biblical revelation was coalescing in my mind, and I could perceive a cable of continuity between Old Testament prophecies and New Testament accounts of the life of Jesus Christ. Pouring over Go texts and diagrams supported the same flavor as scouring concordances and lexicons for eschatological nuances in Biblical language. I recalled my homemade koine Greek flashcards, and approached Go with the same fervor of attention. Sometimes the subject of study is less important than the studying itself—the discipline, the healthy exercise of mind, the application of patience and will, the edifying trance.

I also savored Go from my perspective as a professional wildland firefighter. Often the basic aim of a wildfire incident commander is to surround territory with a secure control line, and, like a Go player, he or she must extend that territory from a strong base. In fire suppression it's called an anchor point, and might be a roadway, body of water, rockslide, or previously burned ground. Any Go master would implicitly understand the danger and potential futility of constructing a fireline without an anchor point.

Go is a battle game, and the terminology is evocative of violence and war. From the index of our Go manual: *ko threat, tiger's mouth, attacking, killing, knight's move, invasion, capturing races, dead stones*. A Go player is a general, or perhaps a warlord. With the possible exception of sex, I can think of nothing more celebrated by humanity than warfare. As an American male growing up in the 1950s and '60s—in the thrall of the Cold War and Vietnam—I was pressured by television, school, and the cultural milieu to be a soldier, and war games, both indoor and outdoor, were my chief form of childhood play: "Dogfight," "Battleship," "Beachhead," "Risk," and simply "War."

Thus for all these reasons I was captivated by Go, enmeshed in a fascination/frustration relationship aimed at becoming more cunning. I battered at the walls of my mental limitations and the high ramparts of the game itself, intimidated by its two-thousand-year history. I was reminded of our upwind struggle across the ice, pumping ahead against the cold blast, but relishing the expectation of turning to fly down the lake with the gusts at our backs. That's how I felt each time I suddenly recognized the implications of a specific shape in the latticework of deployed stones. I was pleased to the point of exhilaration.

However, there was also rage and black disappointment, and I was surprised and frankly frightened by the emotional intensity.

Whenever I made a stupid, reckless, or ignorant move and its consequences (lost stones and territory) became evident, my anger soared—not with my opponent, but with myself. I felt utter disgust, even self-contempt. I was investing so much time, effort, and affection into the game that it was growing important in my life and, because of its difficulty, increasingly vital to my self-esteem. Part of the rage was triggered by cruel surprise. The patterns of stones are insidious in that often what appears to be your advantage is in reality your downfall. As you sit intent on your own designs, the carefully crafted shapes of an adversary are literally invisible, and when she plays the stone that seals the fate of one of your "armies," the reaction is shock. "I didn't see it!" Followed by boiling indignation that you could be so dense—after all that practice!

This was ugly. Bad. Not only for my blood pressure, but for my game. In the manual, under the heading "Go Etiquette" are listed some of the precepts of proper play: " . . . good manners . . . be calm . . . make the best of mistakes [which I interpreted two ways]   be a gracious winner and a graceful loser." The path was summed up by a single pithy statement: "Go etiquette is functional and straightforward, and has a tendency to improve your play."

My frustration and anger were violating that good sense, and I knew I needed to break my obsessive approach to Go. I needed to view it as many Asians do—as an art rather than a game.

I am familiar with obsessive-compulsive behavior, and while not clinically mentally ill—at least not yet—I acknowledge the tendencies in my life. It's not all bad. Minor obsessions and compulsions help accomplish a mound of useful work. Obsession overcomes inertia almost every time: the firewood gets split in sufficient quantity in a timely fashion, writing assignments are turned in ahead of deadline, my fire engine is always ready. But . . .

I'm also an avid Nordic skier. Friends will snicker to read that. No, they'll say, you're a *fanatical* Nordic skier. A couple of years ago I skied 126 days in a row (averaging about five miles per day), and but for a spell of fever and chills that forced me into bed, would have tallied close to 150. On balance, I enjoy cross-country skiing immensely, but admittedly *not every day*. On many occasions during that long winter I would've been content to skip my five-mile jaunt. In fact, I sometimes forced myself out the door. It wasn't the skiing per se that drove me—it was *the streak*, the mounting total of days-in-a-row, and the overpowering compulsion to keep extending it. There seems an inherent satisfaction in counting, and to that end I skied in any weather—subzero cold when the snow was like sandpaper and my toes numbed; late-season sunshine when the track was mush and I actually poled through puddles; during blizzards when I broke trail through calf-deep drifts. Avid? Oh yes. Clearly my skiing transcended fun and exercise and mutated into what some might consider weirdness. But I pushed on to the bitter end, until there was more mud than snow, and I simply had to stop or wreck my skis.

As my two-month obsession with Go was peaking, I had skied 65 days in a row, and one afternoon in late January as I swept along a local ski trail, I realized that given the remarkable snow accumulation of that winter, it was probable I could break the 126-day record. A 140-day streak was "reasonably" within reach. I felt a tingle of excitement.

But that evening, during a Go game with Pam, I failed to notice an obvious weakness in an arrangement of my stones, and she was able to deliver a blow that probably cost me the match. I was stupefied, then furious. I castigated myself severely, out loud. My voice was an alarming hiss. Pam drew back and cocked an eyebrow. "Are you having fun?" she asked.

Well, certainly not at that moment. I was ashamed. Such anger was not only a violation of Go etiquette, but simply childish. It was disturbing to Pam, and toxic to the warm and loving atmosphere engendered by a game board on our kitchen table, with the woodstove's glow reflected in windows and soft music from the stereo lapping at the log walls.

I realized I needed to blunt the obsession, the source of the rage. I also recognized the link between the immersion in Go and the compulsion to tally consecutive ski days. The goals were different, but the issue of unhealthy self-control was the same.

From long experience I knew that resisting a specific compulsion—like amassing personal skiing records—caused stress, an annoying tension that was instantly alleviated by giving in to the urge. (Another reason, I suppose, that skiing felt so good.) It's a cyclic phenomenon, building and releasing throughout each day, and it was that cycle of compelling habit that I needed to break. If I could conquer the skiing, I reasoned, then perhaps I could also master the unwholesome aspects of my Go fixation. I was determined, therefore, that the next day I would not ski.

It was -50 degrees F in the morning—Groundhog Day—and an all-time low temperature record for Minnesota of -60 was set in Tower, a town about thirty-five miles away. But I suspected it might be even colder down in the bog west of our cabin, so just before sunrise I hiked down the hill with a thermometer. I could feel the drastic change of temperature on my face, and it was impossible to take a deep breath without coughing. In the flat of the bog, amidst scattered black spruce and tamarack, I set the thermometer atop the snowpack. I watched in wonder as the mercury dropped to -65, then separated into discrete bands of fluid. The bulk of it settled a smidgen below -70. I spit into the air, but it did not freeze before it hit the snow. So much for Jack London.

I remembered my promise to eschew skiing that day, and I chuckled. Such extreme cold (the afternoon high surged to -20) certainly made it easier to stay indoors. To counteract that advantage, I snowshoed for a mile and a half at around noon—out to a beaver lodge on a nearby lake. There. That proved it wasn't the cold that kept me off the skis, but sheer force of will.

Nevertheless, the day wasn't over, and the urge to ski nagged at me with the pervasive insistence of a need—like a yearning for caffeine, nicotine, or sugar. Even after dark I eyed the gibbous moon and noted there was more than enough light to negotiate the trails. Fortunately we had a dinner engagement with friends, followed by an art show opening at a gallery in town, and by the time we got home it was relatively easy to let the few minutes until midnight slip away. The new skiing streak was broken at 65 days. Unlike succumbing to the compulsion, resisting brought no palpable relief, only an anemic intellectual satisfaction.

But before bed I grasped a handful of Go stones and ordered myself to accomplish the same task with the game—disrupt the cycle of need. It helps to speak this brand of self-direction aloud.

I determined that from now on I will regard the game/art of Go in the spirit outlined by a quote attributed to the Chinese philosopher Lao-tzu: "When armies are mobilized and issues joined, the man who is sorry over the fact will win."

I will approach the board and stones with an air of benign regret and eager reluctance. Even if—after years of practice—I manage to decipher the deepest intricacies of the game, I will play the stones with firm humility, making only the best of mistakes. Above all, I will remember that there was a late-November evening when all I expected after ice skating was a cup of hot chocolate and the companionship of friends, and that a casual query drew me into battle. It was not unlike being paged to a fire.

And oh yes, it turns out that if I hadn't broken that ski streak at 65 days, the snow cover was such that I could've tallied at least 146 days. Damn.

CHAPTER EIGHT

Epicedium

All things move in music and write it.
The mouse, lizard, and grasshopper sing together on the
Turlock sands, sing with the morning stars.

John Muir

In June 1996 my Minnesota fire crew was dispatched to northwest Ontario, where over two-hundred fires were ignited in a matter of hours, chiefly by lightning. Canadian fire crews were quickly deployed and fully tapped, and the Ontario Ministry of Natural Resources requested our help.

There's an exalted psychological zone familiar to wildland firefighters involved in "project fires," the long, brutish campaigns that often unfold far from home. As a veteran of many such operations, I've been privileged to reach a lofty plane of blissful fatigue several times.

It's a grade of weariness more potent than vigor, a sublime, mind-altering exhaustion—an energized repose akin to meditation that is not easily attained. I suspect there are some in contemporary Western society who pass entire lifespans never knowing its elation. Perhaps when they were children, in summer.

The weariness dilates for days or weeks, the result of extreme physical exertion, sleep deprivation, and sustained acuteness of mind, perhaps spiced with occasional danger. But in Ontario I was elevated to a strange new sphere.

Our twenty-person unit was assigned to a five-thousand-hectare fire near the remote hamlet of Graham, about eighty miles north of the border. When we arrived, a Canadian fire crew was installing a pair of roof-mounted sprinklers on every one of a few dozen houses (mostly summer cottages). The residents had been evacuated. If the fire overran the community, lakeside pumps would generate artificial rainfall to shield the structures.

Our mission was to establish a fire control line designed to blunt the threat to Graham; and as soon as helicopters were available, we were flown to a bog at the north end of the fire. My four-person squad was first-in, and as the Bell 204 settled into the muskeg on its tundra pads, we slid open the doors, letting in the sweet aroma of conifer smoke and a voracious horde of mosquitoes and blackflies. We were deep in the north woods, and for the next sixteen days it was home—canvas tents, cookstoves, and the brush for a latrine.

We off-loaded a Mark-3 pump, handtools, and six backpacks of hose, then crouched in spongy sphagnum as the helicopter lifted away. It was an initial attack on uncontrolled fire edge, so we launched our assault in earnest, barging through alder brush and thickets of young jackpine with the sixty-pound packs, one-and-a-half-inch hose playing out as we lunged through "the jungle."

In twenty minutes we deployed over a thousand feet of hose, snuffing flame with a smooth-bore nozzle. In two hours of relentless labor we established nearly a quarter-mile of secure line, stringing another thousand feet of hose as we advanced into a stand of mature jackpine and white spruce. The Canadians were pleased, but it was only the beginning. For the next two weeks we slugged it out with the fire, from dawn till dusk, fifteen-hour days in the solstice season of high noons and long, flushed twilights.

During the campaign we endured the cruel gamut of a northern June—from shivering frosty mornings to a brain-stewing 97° afternoon; from dusty, sinus-parching wind to cold drizzle and mud. We labored through it all, our necks swelling with blackfly stings.

On June 28, a violent thunderstorm lashed in at midafternoon, and my squad watched in wonder as a black roll cloud riven by lightning and shoved by tree-spinning gusts convulsed the sky. Tony, whooping with joy, was so exhilarated by the show that he stripped off his clothes and danced in the puddles produced by the downpour.

Ryan shook his head. "He's crazy!"

"No, I don't think so," I replied.

On June 29, our sixteenth day in the bush, my squad hunted for lingering hot spots and rolled up several thousand feet of dirty hose. As usual, we earned our wages, and the day's burden was compounded by latent fatigue from the previous fifteen shifts.

By late afternoon we were back in camp, a meadow speckled with yarrow and daisies. I dropped my web gear and helmet near our tent and laid in the grass. I plucked a stalk and chewed on the green sweetness of summer as an hors-d'oeuvre. Another squad was cooking supper. To the east and north I watched a bank of tumid cumulus clouds, blue-gray at the base and dyed orange above, their high thunderhead anvils fringed in pink and magenta. Every few seconds the distant cloud mass flashed into electric white translucence, the sunset hues burned away by lightning. At the edge of the meadow a dense forest canopy supported the sky with spires of spruce, and on the evening breeze I smelled the cold expanse of Graham Lake.

And from that far-north water, in counterpoint to the desultory conversation of comrades, wafted the melody of loon song, a wild serenade of tremelos and yodels. I felt the clear notes thrum my chest. Sensitized to beauty by righteous weariness, I was enchanted—gently bullied by the grand tableau of sky, sunlight, and forest. With my physical frame sapped and subdued, my spirit soared, freed by the enforced peacefulness of a chastened body, not shunted aside by hormonal demands of action—the chemical static of fight and flight.

I suddenly felt hopeful, confident of the future and charged with a celebratory anticipation. Of what? Everything and nothing. Life was good.

Then, from across the lake, at the rim of awareness and so faint at first that I wasn't sure I heard it, came other music.

Bagpipes.

The aeriform notes seemed woven into the breeze—like the soft moaning of pine needles—gradually growing louder, and my neck tingled. I sprang up, reenergized—like Tony cavorting in the deluge—and took three or four steps toward the distant pipes. A nearby comrade said, "What is it?" I shushed him with a violent wave. "Listen! Bagpipes."

I took a few more steps and froze, perked up like a retriever. It was the most stirring and romantic music I'd ever heard. Small wonder that pipers formed the vanguard of armies, marching into the maw of muskets and bayonets with terrible orphic splendor. I felt summoned. I felt ready for anything. For a moment.

Abruptly the music ceased. I stood alone at the edge of camp, willing it to resume. It didn't. But I had been transported, resurrected from sublime fatigue to a higher level of awareness.

I felt an aching yen to preserve the event, to keep it handy, filed, and so vibrantly fresh that when I needed it, the entire episode would unfurl and be—a virtual replay of reality, a utilitarian hallucination. An antidepressant. A painkiller. A stimulant. A psalm.

But to guard its purity I'd be able to wield it just once: at the moment of death. It was manifest, I saw it: my dying was serene, announced by bagpipes as I lay in grass—hands folded, face open to the sky. Later the mourners/celebrants danced naked in the rain.

I wished for it to happen—someday. I turned and eased back into the midst of camp and colleagues. For now, I needed supper and a good night's sleep.

CHAPTER NINE

Their Eyes, Their Lives

*Take care of the sense and the sounds
will take care of themselves.*

Lewis Carroll

Did the stark contrast of chalk on blackboard adjust my vision? I don't know. But when I turned to face the class I truly witnessed their eyes for the first time—like seventy pairs of tiny sparks. That, and the fact that my illustrated anecdote had jolted them. The sparks were bright. Some mouths were ajar. No one was dozing.

Vitality radiates from human eyes. When pupils are intent and engaged, a steely feedback loop of enthusiasm courses from optic nerve to optic nerve, fusing a nexus between teacher and students. It's a satisfying moment for all.

I felt privileged to be in front of these men and women, lecturing about wildland fire fighting. Most were rookies, young enough to be my offspring. That startles me. I don't feel like a father figure. These "youngsters" clearly wanted to be what I am—an experienced itinerant firefighter, a grizzled freelance familiar with the fuel types of half the United States and Canada. I was appropriately flattered. There are numerous professions in modern industrialized society that do not ignite envy or desire in the young, and I've lived some: sewage plant operator, door-to-door salesman, fast-food cook, logger. Most jobs, in fact, suck. These students understood that.

What the majority didn't yet realize is that wildland fire fighting mainly sucks too—it's 90 percent drudgery and tedium. But the other 10 percent is a beguiling blend of joy, terror, honor, and love that can reliably provide the peak experiences of a lifetime. Often the work is even useful.

A prominent factor in the fire service equation is comradeship. Shared suffering and shared triumph are sturdy bonding agents, and a good fire crew doing good work is a happy band, an extended family of cousins that cares for its own and laughs a lot. I reappear for the punishment season after season because the inevitable pain—both physical and emotional—is eclipsed by the zest of fellowship sweetened by hardship and combat. I'm also paid.

A notable aspect of teaching is its capacity for inflicting humility. At one point during the week-long course, I projected a certain slide. It was an aerial photo of the incipient stage of an actual local fire from a few years before, an excellent overview of the fireground that displayed access, fuels, structures threatened, wind direction, and so on—most of the information required for an incident commander to make the all-important first decisions about suppression resources and tactics.

Employing a pointer and a self-assured tone, I outlined the variables and my preferred plan of initial attack. It sounded good until a young woman raised her hand and revealed that as a member of a volunteer fire department she'd been dispatched to that particular blaze. It was one of her first wildfires, and she graciously informed us what actual tactics had been used, and how the operation had successfully unfolded. Her account and my proposals did not mesh. My plan would've worked—probably—but I was humbled. Again. The classroom is a safe place for miscues and enlightenment, and I was grateful—really. There is nothing deadlier than uninformed certainty. Taped to the wall next to my desk is a quote I clipped out of a fire service trade journal: *Their lives depend on your leadership.*

Now that I had their eyes, that sobering *bon mot* hung before me as if it were shimmering in the air. Slightly edited: *Their lives depend on your instruction.* It would've been simple to dismiss that as too melodramatic, too seductively self-important for one fire class and one fire instructor. But effective instruction—that is, communication—is based on trust. Trust is grounded in commitment. To that end, I did the students no disservice by briefly assuming responsibility for their lives. I matched their collective gaze with an easy intensity, with a commitment that begged no conjuring. It was apparent to them that I had "been there." They should listen.

Except for Sara. She couldn't hear.

Before the first class I was stunned by the news that one of the students was deaf. Greg, our course coordinator—sounding taxed and chagrined—informed me that the young woman, an employee of the Minnesota Conservation Corps, would be accompanied by two sign-language interpreters who would share the stage with the instructors.

I was incredulous. I raised pragmatic objections to a severely hearing-impaired person on the fireground, and Greg interrupted, "I know, I know—tell me about it! I questioned it. But the State says we have to train her—the Americans with Disabilities Act."

Well, OK. I resolved to reconsider my knee-jerk reaction. Think about it, I told myself, write it all down.

I did. And the more I considered the notion, the more dangerous and ill-conceived it seemed. Throughout the week, my keystone message was the importance of communications on the fireground—not only for the coordinated implementation of tactics and strategy, but also for firefighter safety and survival. For starters, Sara couldn't use a radio, arguably the most important tool out there; she couldn't hear shouted warnings or commands;

couldn't discern the approach of bulldozers or helicopters, or note the change in pitch of a working pump or motor that can convey so much valuable, even critical, information. I imagined her trying to dig line on a twenty-person handcrew, or helping to deploy a long, complicated hoselay—dynamic activities dependent on synchronized effort controlled by verbal commands, and often done at night. Reading lips would be impractical or impossible. Even if she was provided with a firefighter shadow fluent in sign language (an unlikely prospect), the process of ensuring that she got the messages would be too sluggish and cumbersome, and hence dangerous. A crew boss or incident commander, already burdened with concerns, could not be faulted for viewing her as a liability—in effect, as an injured firefighter who required special care.

I wondered if the tag team of interpreters (they regularly spelled each other, and I could see it was hard work) would be a distraction, but after a few minutes in class I forgot about them. I was fascinated though, as I watched them perform for other instructors. I picked up a little sign language and noted that not only were they translating, they were also editing and improvising. An awkward locution by an instructor was cleaned up and clarified; an unfamiliar technical description was briefly acted out, and I grinned at their workaday mime. Occasionally one of the interpreters would approach us after a session to make sure they understood a concept or definition, then duly emphasized it to Sara. I relished the irony that it was possible she was deriving more from the course than any of the nonhandicapped students. This suspicion was supported by her keen attentiveness and by the fact that she aced most of the written exams.

Still, the classroom was literally academic, bearing little relationship to an actual fireground. Since she was obviously intelligent, I made it my mission to prove to her—while teaching the others—that she didn't belong on an operational fire crew. Surely she would see that. Presumably no one was more aware of her limitations than she.

And on this last day of the course that was the theme: limitations. The title of the class was "Standards for Survival," concentrating on the "18 Watchout Situations" and the "10 Standard Fire Orders." To give you a flavor, two of the Watchout Situations are #3, *Safety zones and escape routes are not identified*, and #8, *You are constructing a line without a safe anchor point.* Two of the Fire Orders are #1, *Fight fire aggressively but provide for safety first*, and #5, *Remain in communication with crew members, your supervisor, and adjoining forces.*

I hammered at the point that of the more than four-hundred wildland firefighter fatalities since 1926, a disproportionate number were due to overconfidence or arrogance that led to flawed decisions and questionable actions. There might be a time and place to be gung ho, and *esprit de corps* is fine and necessary as long as it doesn't generate a supply order for body bags. Burned firefighters are ugly firefighters. No one can expect you to do any more than your best, and the best should make it home. We are fallible, flesh-and-blood human beings, and we cannot breathe fire or save everything and everybody. The number-one priority is firefighter safety and survival because if firefighters are dropping like flies, they can't help anyone else. Amidst the tightly knit sinews of a fire crew and the complex interactions on the fireground, you automatically take care of others when you take care of yourself.

A mortal sin, I told them, is to *carelessly* transform yourself from an asset to a liability. When a firefighter goes down, he or she becomes a priority and the operation suffers. In one sense, to be hurt is to be self-indulgent.

All teachers flirt with hypocrisy occasionally, facing the hoary contretemps of "do as I say, not as I do." While preparing my homily about fire-fighting sins, I recalled an incident from four years before. Our volunteer fire department responded to an early morning blaze at a resort cabin. Flames were lapping at the eaves from two windows when we arrived. While leading an interior attack, laden with wet turnout gear, a SCBA, and an inch-and-three-quarter hoseline, I felt a dagger of pain in my right knee. Something crucial had given way. I was scared, but also rueful: if I'd proposed a hypothetical question—"where might be the worst place to puff a knee?"—near the head of my list would've been "inside a burning building."

Though hurting, the knee seemed more or less functional, and as I limped out of the cabin after we knocked down the fire, I was hopeful. Maybe the injury wasn't serious after all.

Several hours later, lying on the living-room floor in front of the woodstove, I absently stretched my right leg. I bellowed. It was like an electrocution, a fierce spasm of pain that locked up my knee joint. I writhed on the floor as Pam anxiously hovered, asking if there was anything she could do. Nope. Gradually, excruciatingly, the knee unlocked.

Over the next couple weeks, two orthopedists diagnosed a torn meniscus and recommended surgery. I resisted. The knee was feeling pretty good. I could walk, jog, ski, and even successfully worked another structure fire. Why endure the risk, suffering, and expense of surgery?

But one of the doctors, aware of my vocation, said, "Your knee *will* lock up again. What if it happens at a critical moment on a fire?"

Of course he was right, and I was ashamed of my selfishness and cowardice. As much as I dreaded surgery, I owed it to my colleagues. To avoid the operating room would be a dereliction of duty. In this case, pain was righteous, and confronting the needles and cutters was no less than mandatory.

That was how I wanted Sara to feel: to be acutely aware that her condition was a liability and a threat to her would-be colleagues. In her case, the single important duty she could perform as a trained rookie firefighter would be to never fight a fire.

Some might argue that this was intimidation. Subtle, perhaps—even well-meaning—but intimidation nevertheless. Others might say it even represented the arrogance I deplore—via a unilateral determination that someone was unfit. I prefer to think of it as prudence informed by experience and guided by a sense of responsibility. And every instructor realizes that a dose of intimidation can be a trenchant teaching device, especially if the instruction concerns matters of life and death. I was seeking to modify behavior, and there are two basic means: the carrot or the stick. I figure, use the stick of intimidation during fire instruction, but do it with respect; scare them out of love.

The grand finale of the Standards for Survival class is an introduction to fire shelters followed by a shelter deployment drill. A fire shelter is basically a reinforced aluminum-foil pup tent. If firefighters are about to be entrapped and overrun by a fire, they are to shake open the shelter, snuggle inside, hold on tight, and hope for the best. The foil reflects 95 percent of the radiant heat, and shelters are credited with saving about 250 lives since they were introduced a couple of decades ago. My main goal was to emphasize that (1) shelters are not foolproof; it's possible to die inside one; and (2) it's far better to be savvy enough to avoid an entrapment in the first place. I made these points as vividly as I could, demonstrated the proper deployment of a shelter, then readied them for intimidation.

I separated the class into "crews" of twenty, each person outfitted with gloves, web gear, and a practice fire shelter. As the first crew came nervously forward, I outlined the scenario. They were on a ridgetop, about to be overrun by flames. I pointed to the west end of the hall and said that was "downslope," where the "fire" was coming from. They should deploy the shelter so their feet faced that way. The doctrine: it's better to burn your feet than your head. Two of my fellow instructors drifted through the crew checking gear, and I held up my watch.

"You've got twenty-five seconds to get under the shelter. Everyone ready? . . . Go!"

Then my colleagues and I were screaming at them: "Let's go! The fire's coming! Let's *go*! It's getting hot! Move! Move!"

There was a lot of jerking and fumbling. They were rattled. From my own student experiences I know that drills—even utterly safe ones such as this—can generate high stress and honest, pulse-throbbing fear. Our shouting was designed to maximize bedlam, providing the impediments to performance that might be manifest during a real burnover. We didn't want our students to fail per se, but rather to glean at least an inkling of how difficult a fire shelter deployment can be and to understand the necessity of further practice. Most of them required a lot more than twenty-five seconds, and many of the shelters were not properly deployed. I stalked amidst the tents, tugging at the peaks. "Here's the wind!" I'd shout, and a slight jerk exposed their legs. I'd grab their foot and say, "This is burning! You've got to hold these shelters down."

When everyone was finally tucked and settled, ensconced in their dark and stuffy little cosmos with hearts racing, I said, "Remember, you may have to remain in your shelter for hours." Then I shut up and let them think about that. I hoped they all were scared, that they realized they needed more work.

In the controlled frenzy of the drill, I didn't pay particular attention to Sara, but I hoped she had learned enough to make a wise decision about fire fighting. Those who have survived actual entrapments accent the need for people to communicate while they're inside shelters—chattering encouragement to keep panic at bay as heat rises to intensely uncomfortable levels. In the shelter training manual it says: "During entrapment, talk to other trapped firefighters by radio or shout back and forth . . . Talking helps relieve stress . . . " A possibly life-saving technique that Sara would be unable to employ—another strike against her.

When the practice shelters were neatly stowed and the students back in their seats, I delivered my closing pitch. I reminded them that within the Incident Command System there are people whose job description includes watching after the welfare of firefighters—squad leaders, crew bosses, safety officers—at one level or another just about everyone out there.

"*But*," I said, "in the final analysis, *you* must take responsibility for your own well-being."

Some heads nodded in assent. It's a simple concept. But as my gaze swept the room for the last time I knew that some of them, perhaps even those nodding, didn't really get it. The full import of *personal responsibility* would only dawn via hard testing on the fireground—in the midst of some battle where there were no daddies, no mommies, and no teachers with chalk. I hoped their colleagues would be true comrades.

"Well, maybe I'll see you out there," I said. "Good luck."

There was a round of applause, and I bowed my head in acknowledgment and embarrassment, fiddling with papers. Their eyes were too charged, too trusting. They were scaring *me* now. A lot of teaching is performance, with classroom as theater, and I wanted this final act to remain vivid in their minds, and myself to disappear. To be applauded doesn't necessarily mean you've succeeded.

Six weeks later there was a fierce wildfire in northern Minnesota, and Greg, our class coordinator, was in command. He requested additional crews, and the MCC was tapped. By coincidence, Sara's crew was dispatched, and Greg was notified of her impending arrival. Isn't it strange how some episodes run full circle? But the action that wasn't politically feasible during our training session was now just a matter of fiat. Greg, as incident commander, simply refused to allow Sara on the fireground. No one objected. She never fought a fire.

CHAPTER TEN

Totem

*A man must be a little mad if he does not want
to be even more stupid.*

Michel de Montaigne

A red squirrel dashed out of some goldenrod by the side of the road and directly beneath the left front tire of my truck. If I hadn't seen the flash of fur and tail, I wouldn't have noticed the subtle thump that signified its death.

I checked the rearview mirror and saw the squirrel lying near the centerline, twitching. Damn. I slowed, preparing to back up and at least finish it off. But before I stopped, and less than ten seconds after the hit, a raven swooped out of an aspen tree just ahead and to the left. A witness. It flapped over to another aspen above the squirrel and paused for a moment, then dropped to the highway and hopped twice to reach my victim. The meat was still warm, the blood hot. The raven began to peck.

I didn't believe for an instant that the raven was there by coincidence. Its manner was casual, workaday. They are shrewd birds, well aware of the deadly bounty provided by the interaction of vehicles, asphalt, and wildlife. A tall aspen off the shoulder of

Greenrock Road is an excellent spot for a raven to hang out—roadkill buffet.

My guilt at squashing the squirrel was partially assuaged. I had inadvertently served a fresh meal to a raven, and ravens are my allies.

I discovered this while brushing a hiking trail near Gunflint Lake for the US Forest Service. My boss and I fell into conversation during a break, and I asked him about a curious design he'd drawn on the front of his shirt. It was three pairs of short zigzag lines, and he said it was a stylized symbol of his personal totem—ripples on water. He'd recently attended a seminar where an artist had encouraged students to unveil their totems by recalling their earliest memory and then meditating on it via writing, drawing, free association, whatever. The meaning of the recollection would eventually assert itself, and a specific totem would emerge. He explained that his earliest childhood memory was a vivid image of his mother's coffee cup—brimming and just set down on a tabletop. He remembered the sunlit ripples on the surface.

As it happened, I'd read about totems the evening before, in a book of Native American history. Originally, especially among the Algonquin branch of tribes, totems (such as a bear, wolf, or loon) were appropriated by clans and families rather than by individuals. They were symbolic badges, roughly equivalent to European coats-of-arms, and employed to determine kinship and protect bloodlines. For example, people of the same totem did not intermarry.

Personal totems seem to be a function of the New Age movement, a modern revival of non-Judeo-Christian philosophy and religious practice that isn't always true to its supposed roots. While acknowledging this distinction, I was nevertheless enamored of the idea of a personal symbol, and a couple of weeks later I sat down to explore the totemic aspects of my oldest memory.

Though over forty years past, it's a lucid recollection: a black ether mask being placed over my face prior to surgery at age two.

My blade of topiary thought sculpted the idea of anesthesia into symbolic death—unconsciousness, no pain—initiated by a black messenger (the mask). I immediately thought of a raven, a bird that folklore considers not only to be a messenger, but also to represent creative power, solitude, spiritual strength, and prophecy.* Ravens are also associated with beginnings, and the black mask/messenger was the literal birth of my mind—as I remember it. Besides, ravens have long been my favorite bird, admired for their beauty, boldness, and intelligence.

Thus I had my personal totem. So what? Did it change my life? Not in a momentous way. But any time we establish another nexus to a phenomenon or entity outside ourselves, we enhance the quality of our lives and deepen the reservoir of our minds.

"Nature speaks in symbols and in signs," wrote the poet John Greenleaf Whittier, and his contemporary Emerson was more emphatic: "We are symbols and we inhabit symbols."

When I see or hear (or dream about) ravens, the experience is automatically significant. I assume a link with ravens and their symbolic values, and via imagination ascribe importance to the encounter. I manufacture meaning. And it works.

For example, on a blustery October afternoon a month after I hit the squirrel, I was walking on a dirt road south of our forty, taking a break from writing. The sky was gradually darkening as a cloud deck clotted ahead of a low-pressure front that promised a storm. The last of the aspen leaves were clipped from their branches and blown away, the final dried fragments of summer tumbling to the forest floor, soon to be buried by snow. The air was damp and cold, suffused with the evocative aroma of late autumn—an intoxicating blend of weathered leaves, cooling lakes, and, faintly, wood smoke.

Before I left the cabin I'd been sweating over a poem. I was stalled, hunting for an image or metaphor to keep the work alive

---

*J. E. Cirlot. *A Dictionary of Symbols*. (New York: Philosophical Library, 1971).

and growing. I decided to drop it for a spell and take the dog for a hike.

At one point we cut into the woods to inspect a dying birch I intended to cut for fuel wood, and as we pushed through a clump of red osier dogwood and back onto the road, I heard a loud cry directly overhead.

Two ravens—wingtip to wingtip—swept past, pushed by the wind. They weren't flapping, but simply riding the violent currents that noticeably ruffled their feathers and pitched them, sideslipping, to the east. Though midnight black, they seemed oddly bright against the ragged gray overcast, almost luminous in contrast to the clouds. They banked in unison and swung out of view over the forest canopy.

A couplet materialized on my lips: "Two ravens soared before the storm/ I thought of you and I."

That was it. In the context of the poem I'd been writing it was perfect, and I knew it must be so because Raven, my totem, my ally, had given me the words. I have never been more certain of poetic lines. A pair of gulls or blue jays wouldn't have cut it. For me, those two ravens were no more accidental than the one that waited in the aspen above Greenrock Road. The favor of the dead squirrel had been returned.

A mind game? Sure. Imagination? Blatantly. But that is the essence of creativity—a joyous interplay of symbols, making much of small and sometimes fleeting, chance impressions. Roadkill for the mind.

CHAPTER ELEVEN

The Gunflint Circle

All I care about is life, struggle, intensity.

Emile Zola

We are expendable. The hierarchy would vehemently disagree, but every time I climb into a helicopter I know it's true.

I love helicopters. I love the fireground. I am willing and able, and I lust for dispatch. But I cannot deny the craziness that pits us against flames, sky, and the risk of early death. And what for? Often very little; to "save" trees and brush, to quench fires that need to burn as desperately as lungs crave breath. Who are we to kill nature's desire for rebirth? Who are we to shatter the cycles of thunderbolts and benevolent drought? At what cost do we thwart the biosphere's elemental urge for heat and awe-full light? Let it burn.

But it's good to be expendable. Sometimes I can't bear the thought of being safe. I volunteer. Send me to your fires. Fly me into smoke and wind, and trees that grab for rotor blades. I'll save your pulpwood and lumber. I'll defend the fiber that makes the tissue that blows your nose and wipes your ass. Why not? It's better than living a normal life. You need me. Societies—ancient and modern, democratic and tyrannical—dictate that someone has to be expendable. Pick me; I volunteer.

June 16, 1995

Bill Schuster phoned me from the Minnesota Interagency Fire Center in Grand Rapids and asked if I was available to fill in for two days on the helitack crew based at Orr airport.

"Just for the weekend," he said. Sure, sounded good.

This was gravy. June is statistically the rainiest month in northern Minnesota, and seasonal DNR firefighters—"smoke chasers"—are rarely on the payroll after Memorial Day. But it was hot—in the eighties and nineties day after bright day, with no significant precipitation.

Only three days before, a trio of us smoke chasers were sent to ignite a prescribed burn near Cook. A wildlife manager used a grease pencil on an aerial photograph to outline the area to be burned. It seemed straightforward. We would run a willow-killing fire through a ten-acre wetland in order to promote sharptail grouse habitat. There was bog on three sides, sphagnum moss that was easily "wet-tracked" with the treads of the J-5 Bombardier that we'd towed to the site. The other flank bordered on fifteen acres of brown grass next to Cook's sewage treatment lagoons. That dry grass would burn like hell if we let fire into it, but the ground was hard and we had full access to the flank with our 4WD fire engine. The flames along that edge would be readily controllable.

After surveying the area from atop the J-5, we split up. Scott would run the Bombardier along the bog edge, reinforcing the wet-track and watching for spot fires across that line. Matt would tend the engine and keep fire out of the parched grass. I would wield a drip torch to systematically light the burn.

We were blessed with a perfect westerly breeze, so I started at the east end of the site to create a backing fire. I dropped a match into a swatch of cattails, then shoved the neck and wick of the torch into the pocket of flame. The thin stream of fuel oil/gasoline mixture ignited with a gratifying flash, and we were in business.

I gradually worked to the west in strips, lighting a swath from one flank to the other, allowing the fire to hotly, killingly, run until it slammed into the black produced by the previous strip, and was thus naturally extinguished. Our plan was to execute a half-dozen or so of these strip fires until about a third to a half of the burn area was black, then proceed to the west end and start a final headfire to rip quickly through the rest of the site.

It was a simple, orthodox procedure, and it worked like a dream until the minute I lit that headfire. It was a classic: the wind shifted ninety degrees. The innocuous, creeping flames that Matt was casually directing along a four-hundred-yard section of the dry grass field were transformed from a mild flanking fire into that same length of shoving, ass-kicking headfire. As flames surged into the grass toward the sewage lagoons and an access road, I was both mortified and amused. The timing was wickedly sublime. At no other moment could we have experienced such nimble and profound disaster.

I snuffed out the drip torch and rushed to the engine. As Matt steered along the line, I strode beside the truck with hose and nozzle, spraying at the base of the flames. Scott hit the other end of the line with the treads and nozzle of the J-5. Even at that point, with the fire out of control, a headfire almost a quarter-mile wide, and just three of us to fight it, I wasn't worried. It was only grass, and we had the tools and experience required to regain the upper hand. The ever-fickle wind had betrayed us, but we had responded quickly and efficiently.

The mere grass, however, was nasty and belligerent. It was thick, matted, and crispier than we guessed. It burned ferociously—so intensely that I had to wrap my Nomex helmet shroud around my neck and face to shield skin from the radiant heat. After we'd wiped out about seventy-five yards of fire, I looked over my shoulder and saw that the line had reignited in three or four spots and was energetically spreading. We backtracked to nail them again, and I knew then we didn't have enough water.

In a few minutes the J-5 and the engine were sucked dry almost simultaneously, and Scott trundled off to draft out of the nearest sewage lagoon. Matt and I pulled pump cans off the engine and continued to hump along the line, furiously working the "trombones" of the cans, which are essentially industrial-strength squirt guns. Full, they weigh about fifty pounds; couple that with 90-degree heat, the hellish ambience of the fire, and extreme heart-thumping exertion, plus heaving lungs contaminated by dense smoke. In fifteen minutes I was racked by impressive pain. At one point the smoke was so thick I dropped to my knees, wheezing and hacking—almost wildly gasping for the cleaner air near the ground. My eyes watered, my nostrils ran, spittle dripped from my chin. My scalp was hot and my temples throbbed. I drained the last of the warm water from my canteen and realized I was rapidly approaching heat stress.

At first, I was encouraged by the grass on the banks of the lagoons. It had been burned about six weeks before and regenerated to a lush green shag. We thought it would be as effective as a wet-track in stopping fire—until I noticed it was openly burning.

Then Scott called on the radio to say he was having trouble priming the J-5's pump and didn't think he'd be able to draft a load of water. That was it. We'd have to bite the bullet and call for help. It's embarrassing and humbling to lose a prescribed burn, and it hurts like hell to publicly acknowledge it. But we had no choice. I radioed the Cook forestry office and requested two engines. They arrived within minutes, and after an hour of further struggle we knocked down the rest of the running fire. Most of the brown grass was black, and the fire had sprinted up to the access road and reburned the south embankment of the lagoons. We released the Cook engines to another fire in the area, sending Matt along to help. Scott and I spent another hour mopping up hot spots, and finally drove away, exhausted and chastened. The boss at Cook forestry had not been happy to have his fire crew directed to our escaped prescribed fire on an afternoon of relatively high potential for wildfires. He was going to have a word with our supervisor.

We returned to the wildlife office and proceeded directly to the area manager with our tale of woe.

"Show me the aerial photo," he said.

We outlined the area blackened by the escaped fire, and the boss looked puzzled.

"But that," he said, "is exactly what should have been done. I wanted that grass burned."

Scott and I stared at each other. The assistant area manager had penciled in the wrong fire perimeter on the photo.

"It's OK that you killed more willows in the bog," said the boss, "but the grass had priority."

Scott and I shook our heads and laughed.

"Well," I said, "it's a damn good thing we couldn't put that fire out." A successful suppression effort on our "escaped" fire would've defeated the purpose we were unaware of. And it turned out that the grass was brown because it had been poisoned—to prepare it for fire. Shit. I wondered what toxins had been in that smoke.

The boss grinned. "So," he said, "getting dry out there?"

We are expendable. I don't seek death on the fireground, and certainly not injury. I'm a professional. Most mishaps are avoidable via alertness and skill, and thus most injuries are manifestations of failure. It is humiliating to transform yourself from an asset to a liability, and out in the woods there are few greater liabilities than a disabled firefighter, or a corpse.

Still, if there's a snag with your name on it, or if somebody else screws up, or if the wind takes on a new career of its own—well, the fireground is not the worst place to die. Sudden, massive trauma is not the worst way to die. Age forty-four is not the worst time to die.

June 17, 1995

I was on the clock as soon as I left the house at 9:00 A.M. It's a forty-mile drive to Orr, and the helicopter and crew were supposed to be available for duty at 10:00 A.M.

I met the pilot, the foreman, and my fellow "backseater," a longtime smoke chaser called Bub. He and I had been together on a twenty-person hand crew at the Snowshoe Fire in east central Oregon in 1990.

We walked over to the helicopter, a Bell 206 Jet Ranger—designated 85BH (Eight-Five-Bravo-Hotel)—and practiced deploying and hooking up the one-hundred-gallon Bambi Bucket, a procedure I hadn't performed in almost a year. When we arrived at a fire, Bub and I would connect the bucket to the belly hook of the ship before shouldering our bladder bags and heading for the line. We sorted out who would do what, then settled into a ready-room mode, waiting for the phone to ring or the radio to squawk.

A dispatch seemed inevitable. The near-solstice sun blazed from a pale, cloudless sky, and the temperature was in the nineties by noon. The humidity was low, and the airport flag snapped in a stiff breeze. It felt like Idaho in August. The previous Saturday I'd taken a weekend hike into the Boundary Waters Wilderness and slept out under the stars on a Minnesota June night. Normally, clouds of mosquitoes would've sucked me dry or driven me mad. The last time I recalled such a bug shortage was during the drought summer of 1988—a lucrative, fondly remembered year for fire grunts.

Shortly after noon we received a call to a grass fire on the south shore of Lake Vermilion, about eighteen miles out. We hustled across the tarmac to 85BH, and as the turbine engine warmed up, Bub and I secured our flight helmets, buckled our seat belts, and plugged our helmet jacks into the intercom avionics. It's a happy ritual performed in the kaleidoscopic shadows cast by spinning rotor blades. We lifted off and cut east down the runway, all eyes scanning the sky for other air traffic.

It was a satisfying flight over Minnesota lake country, but a false alarm. An engine crew reached the scene first and reported that air support was unnecessary. We never even saw the smoke. But no matter, it was flight time. (We don't do helitack because we hate to fly.) On the way back we banked over a well-populated great blue heron rookery in a swamp north of the airstrip, and that made my day. It's a godlike sensation to view a spectacle from the air that would demand effort and suffering to see from the ground.

When I got home that evening I jumped into the lake just after sunset, and the water was barely cool enough to be refreshing. It was definitely fire season, and I had high hopes for Sunday.

We are expendable. And yes, we are party to it. We acquiesce and even cooperate in the promotion of our own potential doom. Fatalism. It springs from the mindset: Can Do. We are warriors and we can beat this fire, any fire. If we fail it's our fault. And keep in mind that heroes do not fail. Death before dishonor

I could not love thee, Dear, so much
Loved I not Honor more.

Try that on your spouse as you saunter out the door with your fire pack. Yet we do it; we believe those lines implicitly.

"What Are They Thinking?" was the headline of a story in the June 21, 1995, edition of the Havre, Montana *Sentinel*. It began: "After 80 years of studying fire, the US Forest Service is studying firefighters—and how to develop the behavioral traits that will keep them alive."

Apparently a workshop was conducted by the Forest Service that included input from psychologists and an airline industry expert who trains cockpit crews in techniques of crisis management. Two of the big questions addressed: Why are fire crews so hesitant to abandon tools and packs when they are about to be burned over? Why are they more likely to try outrunning a fire rather than deploy a fire shelter? A psychologist who studied the mass deaths at Mann Gulch and Storm King Mountain offered the obvious, and no doubt correct, explanation: dropping your gear to either run or take cover in a fire shelter is a clear acknowledgment that you are in very deep shit, but to keep packs and tools "is to remain a firefighter rather than become a victim. You're still in it. You can still fight back."

Can Do. Heroes don't fail. Even if they die. No irony intended.

June 18, 1995

We haunted the airport lounge and the patch of shady lawn outside—reading, napping, telling tales. By 1:00 P.M. it was 98 degrees.

A 911 call came over the radio, paging the DNR and a local volunteer fire department, stating that a running grass/brush fire was thirty feet from a building at a resort on Lake Vermilion.

"Sounds like a helicopter dispatch to me," I said. The pilot nodded and stubbed out his cigarette. I slipped into my Nomex shirt. A moment later the phone rang and sent us to Norwegian Bay.

It took us less than twelve minutes to reach the scene, but the resort was prepared with its own pumps and more than enough citizen volunteers. We saw the last wisp of smoke as a bucket brigade of a dozen people scrambled over the rock outcrop where the fire had burned less an acre of grass and blueberry bushes. The ersatz firefighters, most attired in shorts and swimsuits, waved as we hovered overhead. The DNR engine boss enroute informed us that we could return to base.

"Well," the foreman said over the intercom, "we're getting closer. I saw smoke that time."

The pilot banked away and dove for the lake, leveling off about forty feet from the surface then goosing it. We howled down the length of Norwegian Bay at a hundred knots, waving to ogling boaters and anglers, enjoying the delicious rush of raw velocity magnified by our proximity to the waves. Near the end of that three-mile arm of Vermilion, we damn near hit a seagull. It swooped up, saw the ship, then folded its wings and dove away at top speed. We scared the hell out of it. The pilot laughed (I grinned), but if we sucked a gull into the turbine or the rotors, we could be dead meat too, especially so close to the deck: zero room for error. But it was flight time; we didn't strike the gull, and there would be another dispatch. I was certain. It was in the air, in my bones. By the end of the afternoon we'd be sucking smoke and blowing black snot.

An hour later the phone rang again. There was a fire near Hovland, about 125 miles east, not far from the north shore of Lake Superior. We might be dispatched. Stand by.

It seemed unlikely. It would take us an hour to fly there; besides, it was obviously too good to be true. Our projected flight path took us directly over the middle of the Boundary Waters Canoe Area Wilderness, traversing nearly the full length of the 1.2 million acre reserve. To see the BWCAW from the clouds had long been my personal fantasy. A bald eagle's point of view was my ideal, but the backseat of a Jet Ranger would do. We pored over a map of the Superior National Forest, speculating, hoping. Twenty minutes later the phone rang again. The foreman picked it up and listened, scribbling notes. As he hung up he clenched a fist and hissed, "Yes!" I instantly understood two things: the fire was serious, and I wasn't likely to sleep in my own bed that night.

From 3,500 feet the wilderness looked like the surface of a different planet. It was the roads—there were none. The unbroken expanse of forest, lakes, and rivers seemed surreal, and I was momentarily disoriented. It required several seconds to realize that I was gazing at perfection. Not used to that.

I had paddled, hiked, and skied the Boundary Waters on a regular basis since 1965, but had never seen it from the air. The wondrous territory below gradually unfurled like a 3-D map. I knew this country: the Sioux River, Basswood Lake, Snowbank Lake, Gabimichigami, and many dozens of others. I recognized the enchanting, though hard-bitten, realm of the Kekekabic Trail, and in the northern distance saw the sunlit palisades near Stairway Portage and Rose Lake. About a dozen miles east of Ely we skirted the cloudlike smoke column of the Gabbro fire—over one-thousand acres and spreading. It was a lightning-sparked blaze in the wilderness that was being allowed to burn. The prescribed goal was twelve-thousand acres, and we could see flames from five miles away.

At one-hundred knots it took us an hour to traverse the Boundary Waters, and I gained a new appreciation for the scale of its grandeur. My soaring mood verged on the spiritual—that is, I felt excited, fervently reverent, and outside the self. The vast tableau was so magnificent, yet so utterly untouchable, that I had to blink back tears. And I was on the payroll. People wonder why I like firefighting?

I saw our smoke over the foreman's left shoulder, out through the plexiglass bubble, dead ahead. It already had a name—the Devilfish Lake fire—and it was cooking. No one was going to turn us away from this one.

We made an orbit and saw that the fire was centered on a rocky knob, burning fiercely in heavy timber. One flank bordered a small, emerald-tinted lake, but there was no road access. About a mile to the east was a gravel pit, and the pilot eased the ship to a dusty landing in the middle of it.

Bub and I scrambled under the ship to hook up the bucket, and in a few minutes 86BH was off to initiate the airborne water assault. We were the first suppression resources to arrive. A single scout was on the fire, but genuine remoteness was delaying a full-scale ground operation.

Bub and I slung bladder bags over our shoulders, and the foreman grabbed a Pulaski. A DNR forester we'd met at the gravel pit scratched a map in the dirt with his finger, then directed us down a foot trail toward the fireground.

The afternoon heat lay like a heavy wool blanket on the face, and we were soaked in sweat almost immediately. But I was blissful. A long advance through the woods is one of the best parts of the battle. It extends the anticipation and suspense, and until we actually close with the blaze we're more vulnerable—unsure of fire behavior and potential. We were treading a one-way path to a showdown.

We heard the fire before we smelled it. The arousing whoosh of torching conifers and the sharp crackling of incinerated brush indicated robust, voracious burning. The trail angled to the shore of the emerald lake, and there we engaged the flames. It was an ideal spot to establish an anchor point as we fought our way up the right flank, using the lake as a stopper.

We worked in close concert with the ship, directing the pilot's bucket drops onto the hottest sections of the line, then rushing in to back up the hit. Progress was slow—everything was on fire, and tinder-dry deadfalls and snags were reservoirs and ramparts of stubborn heat. A thick carpet of smoldering needle duff and leaf litter made virtually every square yard of ground hot. The smoke was suffocating. My face was quickly blackened and smeared. We edged as close to the helicopter's cascading water as safely possible, shielding our radios and relishing the cold showers at the tail of the bucket drops. We carefully portioned out the five gallons in each bladder bag, spraying only the very edge of the line, where we could actually kill the fire spread.

The terrain was rocky and steep, and I fell once, misjudging the integrity of a small birch snag that I used as a handhold. It broke, but the boulder I struck with my back supported a cushion of moss and I wasn't hurt.

"Careful," said Bub.

I gestured to the burning forest with the overgrown squirt gun I held in my hands, and replied, "Too late for that, man."

After an hour of bucket drops and our dogged ground support, most of the running fire on the right flank was knocked down—that is, significantly slowed, but certainly not completely extinguished. The interior of the fire had consumed the woods cleanly to bedrock in many places, and a twenty-acre swath of forest was a cemetery of snags and charred, crisscrossed deadfalls. Bub and I shook our heads, pitying the mop-up crews. Jumbles of rock and a couple of sheer faces multiplied the hazard, creating an exhausting obstacle course. Many snags had burned-out root systems and were teetering in the wind, primed to topple without warning.

With our bladder bags empty, Bub and I hiked back to our anchor point at the lake. The foreman had already returned to the gravel pit to secure it as a landing spot for 85BH. The ship was low on fuel, and it would be hours before the fuel truck reached us from Orr. A half-dozen DNR and Forest Service firefighters had arrived at the lake with a Mark-3 pump and hose, and we briefed them before heading back to the pit.

About a quarter-mile down the trail I heard a familiar voice up ahead, and a moment later I literally bumped into Mark Adams, a fellow fire bum I hadn't seen for a year—since we'd worked together on a Minnesota DNR handcrew at the Tyee Fire in Washington state. We vigorously clasped hands.

"Hey!" he said, "I thought I heard you on the radio!"

The wildland fire service is a relatively small circle, and that would be proven repeatedly over the course of that wonderful summer. Mark had his trademark Stihl chain saw slung over his shoulder—his sawyer skills are practically legendary—and we chatted briefly before he headed in to begin felling snags.

When we reached the ship the sun was low, and we didn't have much flight time left. We were assigned to stay overnight at a lodge called Naniboujou, on the shore of Lake Superior about twelve miles south of the fire. I had heard of the glories of Naniboujou several years before when a student in one of my creative writing seminars submitted an essay about it. The lodge was built in the 1920s as a private club. The membership hired

Cree artists to decorate the high, vaulted ceiling of the dining room with brilliantly colored images of the Cree pantheon. The essay assured me it was spectacular—like a Native American Sistine Chapel.

Since we didn't know the precise location of the lodge, we flew directly to the North Shore and picked up US Highway 61. The pilot angled in low, following the centerline of the road, and when we sighted a likely looking resort complex, we descended to tree-top level and hovered over the billboard at the end of the driveway. Yup, it read "Naniboujou." We circled the lodge twice in the fading daylight, checking for wires, poles, and other flight hazards, then gently touched down on an expanse of lawn just off the rock beach—still on the payroll. "What a country," said Bub.

Our loud orbits drew a crowd, and stepping out of the ship—rotor blades still spinning and my face stained with soot—was a righteous, job-justifying moment. Lodge guests had heard rumors of the fire, and our unexpected arrival from the sky—like heroes, like gods—was greeted with obvious astonishment and curiosity. The kids were especially entranced. Or so it seemed. Maybe it was only I who was fascinated; given the potent stimulation of the past several hours, my senses were high-pitched and acute, though not necessarily trustworthy. But hell, I *felt* like a god, like Apollo freshly birthed from the clouds. The aura of admiration that hallowed us may have been at least partially fantasy, but even so, I couldn't imagine a more appropriate end to a fire-fighting shift. Except for one more thing: an ice-cold beer.

But to our dismay we soon realized that for all its glory, Naniboujou now caters to a conservative Christian clientele and is alcohol-free. We absorbed this information gracefully, and retired to our rooms to clean up before dinner. Bub and I had just decided who had first dibs on the shower when there was a rap at the door. As I opened it, a middle-aged man shoved a small cooler into my hand.

"Here," he said. "You guys look like you need this."

Inside the cooler, attractively nestled in a bed of crushed ice, were four bottles of Michelob Dark.

"I'll pick up the cooler in the morning," he said, and disappeared down the hall.

Bub and I grinned. Contraband beer—the sweetest brand. Now this, by god, was fire season. And yes, over my steaming bowl of wild rice soup, I noted that the Cree paintings were indeed spectacular.

We are expendable because we are vulnerable. Since we can bleed and die, we will. It is allowed—sometimes encouraged—by the laws of physics, biology, and history. Once we are dispatched to a fire, no one can guarantee our safety or survival. We are frangible, combustible flesh. In 1994, thirty-four of my wildfire colleagues perished in the line of duty. Many hundreds were injured.

But it is unwise and impractical to dwell on the deaths and injuries, and almost no one does. Am I afraid? Yes, but mostly before or after the frightening events. In the heat of battle, I'm usually too busy, too focused, or too awed to notice fear. Afterward, I sometimes shudder and reflect: *we* did *that*? But even the most harrowing experiences gradually evolve into jokes, metaphors, or faded cautionary tales for rookies. Unless, of course, someone was actually killed or maimed. But even then, as time passes, it's just another story.

June 19, 1995
We expected dense, helicopter-eating fog along the Lake Superior coast, but there was none, and we flew back to Devilfish by 8:00 A.M. Bub and I and the foreman hiked back into the fire and tied in with Mark Adams and his Stihl. There was a high, relatively open knob to the north of the main burn, and our mission was to make it a helispot. The fire had remained active during the night, burning over the knob, and we had to pussyfoot over a beaver dam to reach the base of the slope—which was steep, rocky, and

thick with hazel brush and highbush cranberry. Hauling hose and supplies to the knob would be a nightmare, so as soon as we cleared it, 85BH would start flying in gear via cargo nets.

We struggled to the summit by 10:00 A.M., and Mark began to expertly drop the jackpines growing out of the ledgerock crevices. Bub and I cleared away brush and limbs. After about an hour of heavy labor I was satisfied we had a safe spot for slinging cargo, and 85BH could probably land if need be—say, for a medevac.

The next step was to extinguish what fire lingered nearby, and for the next hour we felled and bucked snags and mopped up hot duff with Pulaskis. The noontime heat was relentless, and we soon ran short of drinking water. The foreman had returned to the gravel pit to prepare for the arrival of a second helicopter, and he diverted 85BH from bucket drops to supply us with some bottles of water and Gatorade.

The pilot eased in low and slow from the south, then hovered over the helispot about thirty feet up. I snapped on my goggles, and peering through the cloud of ash and dust kicked up by the rotor wash, I focused on the pilot's right hand sticking out the door.

I let him drop the first plastic bottle to see if it would survive impact on its own. No. The second one bounced off my hands and burst against a rock. On the third drop I perfected the technique that earned us three Gatorades. I half-caught, half-batted the bottles, more or less just breaking their fall. I actually caught the last one, and figured maybe a softball mitt should be kept in the ship. The pilot could toss that out the door first.

We sat on a boulder to savor our airborne beverages, and a few minutes later we saw 85BH lift over the trees with a full bucket. We idly watched as he swung in our direction, assuming he had a target of opportunity in the forest below. But 85BH made a bee-line for our position, and before we thought to budge, the helicopter roared over and the bucket opened. The pilot laid a precise drop on the helispot, literally at our feet. Dust abatement. We were sprinkled by a refreshing mist of trailing droplets. There had been no warning over the radio.

"That show-off!" said Mark, and laughed.

"Yeah," I said, "a real cowboy."

But the helispot was ready.

Mark and Bub were summoned to chain-saw work down near the beaver dam, and I was instructed to stand by on the knob to receive cargo. As I surveyed the neighborhood one more time, I noticed smoke to the north. It was a new, building column, and before I could get on the radio, I heard 85BH call it in. The main fire had apparently delivered a flying ember a quarter-mile to the next dry knob. The pilot swung over, slapped it with a bucket load, and reported that he might not be able to hold it. The fire was burgeoning.

I heard a footfall behind me and turned. A lone firefighter had scaled the knob, and he looked like an authority figure. We shook hands. It was Steve Jakala, a National Park Service fire manager who was the operations chief for the Devilfish. We'd never met, but had spoken on the phone four years earlier when he had offered me a fire-fighting job in Voyageurs National Park. I had gone to Idaho instead.

With a rueful smile, Steve watched the fresh smoke column. "Well," he said, "we've got a new ball game. This thing might hop from knob to knob all the way to Ontario."

Neither of us realized that by the end of the summer, his comment could be touted as prophecy.

Steve studied his map for a moment, then called the ICP in Grand Marais and advised them to close a forest road that ran to the north of the new fire. It seemed to him that road 313 might soon be incorporated into the fireground.

It was also clear that our hard-won helispot was suddenly irrelevant. The Devilfish was mutating to a larger, more voracious beast, and supplies would be needed on the new front. As Steve pushed on to scout the blowup, I descended the knob and retraced our morning route over the beaver dam, across the fire, and back to the gravel pit. It took me almost an hour, and I nearly collapsed. My share of the airborne Gatorade was long gone, and I had a pounding headache that I knew was due to dehydration and heat stress. I felt weak, irritable, and old. Not for the first time I asked myself why I was still punishing myself at age forty-four. I just wanted to find a shady patch of grass and go to sleep. But there was no shade in the pit, so I laid back on a gravel pile and washed down a quick sandwich and a candy bar with two quarts of water, popping a couple of painkillers for dessert. I thought wistfully of Naniboujou and ice-cold Michelob. It was payback time.

A Ryder rental truck had arrived from MIFC, packed with tools and equipment. Bub, our foreman, and I began unloading and establishing a rough inventory, preparing loads in cargo nets that we spread out on the ground.

Our second helicopter arrived in mid-afternoon, another Jet Ranger—56BH, a sister ship to 85BH. As the crew clambered out of the backseat I recognized Tom Schackman, my crew boss at Yellowstone in 1988, and subsequently one of my subordinates at a helibase in Idaho in 1994. It's a small circle. We shared grins and a warm handshake, then rigged 56BH with fifty feet of longline and started shipping hose, pumps, and drinking water out to the line.

In late afternoon, a five-person Minnesota Conservation Corps (MCC) squad arrived from Duluth—eager, but inexperienced. Since there was a lull in cargo operations, I volunteered to walk them in to their assigned sector of the fire. My headache was gone and I'd once again forgotten how old I was, despite sharing the company of rookies who were young enough to be my wayward children.

We followed the same route I'd used that morning, but it had been so radically transformed by bulldozed firelines that my landmarks—certain trees and boulders—were gone. I had hiked out of the fire only six hours before, but when we encountered a junction of three dozer trails, I had to radio a division supervisor for directions. The aggressive advance of the fire—spotting and jumping—had compromised the initial lines and forced construction of new loops that had expanded a simple perimeter into a network. I mused aloud to the MCC people that like society in general, we had too much information. But the squad seemed more intent on the burning snags and the helicopters than on unbidden sociological metaphors from an aging fire bum. Good. The snags were far more pertinent.

June 20, 1995

The morning challenge was to sling-load—that is, fly—a drop tank to the far end of the fire. A drop tank is a collapsible water reservoir—in this case, a 1,500-gallon unit—that can be deployed to remote locations. Out west I've heard them referred to as "bird baths." A plastic liner is affixed to a tubular metal frame, and when the tank is folded up it's rectangular—about eight feet long, two feet wide, and less than a foot thick. That's a rough airfoil shape and thus it wants to "fly," perhaps up into the tail rotor of the helicopter. As with all "wings," the trick is to control that yen for flight.

John, the pilot of 56BH, was skeptical, but I'd dealt with soaring drop tanks in Idaho and was confident I could rig it for a relatively stable journey. I hooked a lead line to each end of the tank and brought the bull rings to a single hook-and-swivel, so that the tank and lines described a triangle. I had another firefighter cut a small balsam fir, about four feet tall, and we used parachute cord and fiber tape to lash the tree to one end of the tank. That was the stabilizer. Aircraft and birds have tails, and so must a flying drop tank.

As the helicopter ascended and the cables tightened, the tank rose to an upright posture and thus cut (more or less) through the air. It couldn't wildly sway or wander, and would certainly stay clear of the tail boom. As the ship swung for the fire, John came on the radio:

"Good job, guys."

It's always sweet to dispel the doubt of professionals.

During the heat of the day I volunteered to pack in a load of fresh fruit and cold drinks to that same far end of the fire, and during the hike in I witnessed my first bulldozer medevac. One of the MCC rookies I'd guided in the previous afternoon had injured her knee, and was perched behind the dozer operator, cushioned by a bunched up cargo net. She was in obvious pain, and the operator was creeping the big Caterpillar down the rough, bouldery line. It was better, I suppose, than tying up four or more firefighters to carry her out, and surely better than her limping out, but I wondered why she hadn't been loaded aboard one of the helicopters. Landing sites were available, especially with dozers around to improve them if necessary. But such decisions weren't mine to make.

At about 3:00 P.M. I cast my fate to a coin toss. A new fire had broken out near Ely, sixty miles west, and a helicopter was requested. It was decided that 56BH would be dispatched along with its foreman, and two helitack were required as crew. Three of us were willing—no, anxious—to go. It's always best to stay fluid on fire duty. It devolved to a coin flip between me and Bub. I won. I happily stowed my gear aboard 56BH, anticipating fresh action. The Devilfish had been a great host, but I'd seen enough. The forest is always blacker somewhere else.

I waved as we lifted out of the gravel pit, relishing a keen sense of déjà vu. But not from real life. This departure was novelistic, cinematic—like a plot twist come alive. I didn't recall a specific

event from a book or movie, but I felt like a *character*, as if playing
the role of heroic protagonist, flying off into the wild blue yonder.

Occasionally I wonder, is this or that image *my* memory or
not; is the event I suddenly remember a thing that really happened to me, or did I just read about it in a particularly engaging
novel? In other words, is the recollection actually someone else's
memory (or dream) now intricately meshed with my own? I suspect that several years hence, when I recall our ascent out of the
Devilfish Lake fire in 56BH, I may wonder, was that real?

Because it was too good, too closely in sync with what we might
have wished. Beyond the joy of dispatch and liftoff was an appreciation for the volatile beauty of the atmosphere. A majestic thunder cell had just slid by to the west, and we skirted its edge on our
way up and out. Nothing lends texture and immanence to the sky
like the billowing topography of cumulo-nimbus clouds and darts
of distant lightning. Such dramatic reference points remind me
that the sky is an *ocean* of air, a writhing sea with "waves" that
sometimes batter what we call our "ship." The ground is the seeth-
ing bottom—jagged and alive, and when we're navigating the realm
of thunderheads and virga, irrelevant.

But only ten minutes or so out of Devilfish we spotted a half-
dozen scattered smokes rising from that living bottom. We flew
directly over one and saw flames running upslope through heavy
timber. These were brand new fires, probably ignited by
downstrikes from the storm cell we'd just dodged. They were all
in the wilderness, and it was questionable whether anyone else
knew of their birth. Yet it seemed incredible that we—who were
already so blessed by the fire gods and a coin toss—were the very
first to spot these blazes. Despite the evidence to the contrary, I
thought that surely Forest Service air patrols had tallied and reported these smokes.

We discussed it over the intercom, and in retrospect our reluctance to go on the air with information about the fires seems curious. But the general drift of reasoning touched on (1) our un-

willingness to believe that we could be in exactly the right place at precisely the right time; (2) a hesitation to jump on the necessary radio frequency (the Superior Forest Net), which was already buzzing with traffic, and where our intrusion might be resented if our information was already known or if the new fires were pegged in the let-burn category anyway; (3) the fact that we were on a specific mission of apparently high priority, and we should mind our own business; and (4) our ability to offer only a rough location for the smokes.

None of these were compelling reasons to keep quiet—indeed I can now think of no compelling reason under the circumstances—but as we flew toward an assigned fire, all twined together and caused us to delay.

Several minutes later, after we'd landed on a wide spot on a remote logging road south of Highway 1 and hooked up the bucket, we were free of the immediacy of dispatch, and our minds cleared. As John flew off to join the two Beavers that were dropping water on the Bogberry Lake Fire, Dean turned to me and said, "Well, I wonder if the Forest Service knows about those fires?"

"We should definitely call them," I said.

Dean radioed Superior Dispatch and described what we'd seen. It was startling news to them, and they diverted a patrol aircraft immediately. In a few minutes we heard radio traffic about initial attack arrangements for some of the fires. It was clear that we should have contacted Superior Dispatch as soon as we saw the smokes, but it was also clear that given their remoteness it was going to take a while for any suppression crews to reach them anyway. We didn't yet realize what these fires would become. Of course, no one else did either.

At about 5:30 P.M., 56BH was released from the Bogberry fire. Dean and I, and Steve, my fellow backseater, had scouted a new helispot—a wider site where the logging road intersected Highway 1—and as Steve and I prepared to halt traffic on the highway, John eased 56BH to a dusty touchdown in front of a stop sign.

We stowed the bucket and flew to the Ely Tanker Base to await a phone call from dispatch.

When the phone finally rang an hour later, we'd concluded we would probably be ordered to fly back to the North Shore to help deal with the new fires. But no, we were to stay in Ely that night, and would receive instructions in the morning. Just before sunset another helicopter—a Hughes 500—arrived to join us in the "staging" mode.

June 21, 1995

We hung around the Ely Tanker Base all morning, chatting with the crew of the Hughs and waiting for another Jet Ranger (55J) that was due in before noon. That one was our ticket out. As soon as it arrived we would be dispatched back east to the Gunflint Trail.

The Jet Ranger landed at about 11:45 A.M., and at 12:15 P.M. we were airborne, headed for the Squat Lake Fire, forty-five miles east-northeast. About twenty minutes later we arrived overhead and saw a Beaver making water sorties to slow the fire's progress until a crew could paddle and portage in. Roughly five acres had been blackened on a steep, rocky peninsula, and we could see no obvious place to land. We made a wide orbit until we found a gravel pit less than two air miles from the fireground, and John eased us in for a landing next to a huge stockpile of crushed rock. Steve and I hooked up the bucket, and 56BH was off to begin drops.

I scaled the stockpile with a stick, shoved it into the "summit," and tied on a length of fluorescent orange ribbon—our wind indicator. No telling how long we'd be stuck there. It was miserably hot, and we were in the process of scouting for nearby shade when a Forest Service engine pulled up.

The driver, a seasonal firefighter named Mark, said that the nearby Seagull Guard Station sported an honest-to-god paved helispot (with shade) only a short drive away, and he'd been sent to ferry us there. We happily tossed our gear into the back of the truck and scampered aboard. I am invariably tickled to leave the unromatic environs of a gravel pit. I left the wind indicator.

The Seagull Helispot was a veritable Cadillac of landing zones. In addition to tarmac, a wind sock, and shade trees, there was a shed filled with helitack supplies, including cargo nets, swivels, and a crash/rescue kit. But the goodies that made our eyes light up were three fifty-five-gallon drums of Jet-A aviation fuel, along with a hand pump and filtering system. Since our fuel truck would require several hours to arrive from Ely, we had already been apprehensive about how long we'd be able to operate. As soon as a fire crew reached Squat—in a couple of hours—they would need to be supplied immediately. By then John would have consumed most of his fuel flying bucket drops.

By late afternoon, the firefighters had established a helispot on the burning peninsula, felling a few pines near a spit of ledgerock on the shore of Squat. Our fuel truck had not arrived. Steve and I wrestled a drum of Jet-A (approximately four-hundred pounds) out of the shed and onto the tarmac with a hand truck, while Dean and John assembled the pump. We threaded the suction end into the larger of the two bungs, pumped some fuel into a clean Mason jar, and presented it to John. He swirled the sample and held it up to the sun. Contamination was obvious, but we figured the black "dregs" had originated in the seldom-used hose, so we stuck the nozzle into the other bung and recirculated fuel through the filter to flush the hose. There is zero tolerance for impurities in turbine fuel. Any water or particulates that reach the engine can cause it to abruptly fail, and no one has yet thought of a convenient time and location for that.

After rinsing the jar, Dean pulled a second sample. John squinted at the fuel, his surrogate lifeblood, and shrugged, "Looks good to me. Pump it."

So while John held the nozzle to the fuel port of 56BH, the rest of us took turns cranking the lever of the hand pump, assuring John that we didn't do windshields and that we were glad he'd be flying alone with the first tank of drum fuel.

"Let us know if the engine quits," said Dean.

John grimaced. "Yeah, right. No problem."

Then we filled some cargo nets and John made the folks on the Squat fire very happy by slinging in a Mark III pump, hose, food, Gatorade, sleeping bags, and, not least—tents. Early reports indicated that the mosquitoes were numerous and apparently famished. There would be no idyllic slumber beneath the constellations.

As for us, we were assigned to a bunkhouse at a Christian summer camp about twenty miles down the Gunflint Trail. It was a slightly ramshackle but homey place called Okontoe. Our hosts were friendly, and our first dinners there were of a decidedly family character—so much so that I overheard another Forest Service guest remark to his companion that "Okontoe" must be the Ojibwe word for "casserole."

But our crew was cheerful. The wilderness was burning and helicopters would be a priority resource. If action was wine, then we'd been welcomed to a bacchanal.

June 22–24, 1995

By 7:30 A.M. we were back at the helispot, ready. For anything. Our official status was blessedly nebulous. The Seagull people kept asking us where we might be sent, and we could only answer that no one at MIFC or any other level of authority was telling us to be elsewhere. While it lasted, we decided to consider ourselves the initial attack ship of the Seagull Guard Station. They were delighted with that, and would see about procuring a chase truck. Due to the proliferation of incidents, the general command and control of fire operations in the Superior National Forest seemed to be in a state of flux, and we were a "rogue ship," staying flexible (fueling out of fifty-five-gallon drums, for heaven's sake) and working in a friendly, informal partnership with local folks. We'd support the Squat fire and be prepared to pounce on anything new.

That this cozy arrangement might soon be upset became clear when we heard radio traffic from the Swede Fire, about eighteen miles southeast. It was one of those we'd spotted on our flight out of Devilfish. The initial attack incident commander informed dispatch that the fire had escaped and requested a heavy helicopter and Type I (hotshot) hand crews. The Superior owned a project fire, and a helibase was sure to follow. That meant 56BH would probably be sucked into the complicated, stressful vortex of a major, multiple-ship helicopter operation. As crew members, we might see our jobs spiral directly into the toilet as we became mere cogs in the helibase machinery, with no fire-suppression duties.

But for the next three days we functioned in two basic modes: wait and respond. We were metaphorically perched on the edge of our seats monitoring the buzz of radio traffic, waiting for someone to call for 56BH—then responding to those calls as swiftly as possible.

We slung more gear and supplies into the Squat fire, and also shipped five additional firefighters. They were members of a Duluth Technical College engine crew, and all but one of them were on their first helicopter flight. I delivered a thorough preflight safety briefing, raising a few eyebrows when I mentioned that they shouldn't be unduly alarmed if the left backdoor of 56BH popped open in flight. The air flow would prevent it from splaying more than an inch or so, and of course all passengers are seatbelted in anyway. Still, it was unnerving the first time it happened to me, and a chronic irritation thereafter. John attempted to repair the door latch temporarily with a heavy-duty rubber band, but it wasn't foolproof, and engendered little peace of mind for passengers. We chided him about ten-thousand-dollar doors that wouldn't stay closed, hoping loudly that such wasn't indicative of the quality of other parts—say, the rotor blades or the turbine, or . . . the pilot.

On the afternoon of June 23 we were dispatched to a new
lightning-caused fire on a ridge above Duncan Lake, less than a
mile south of the Ontario line. It was in wilderness, only a few
hundred yards off the Border Route Hiking Trail. We circled the
smoke, hanging about a hundred feet over the forest canopy, buf-
feted by thermals. A quarter-acre was black, but the running fire
had laid down, smoldering in the duff, awaiting wind. Steve and
I were primed for an assault—a pack-in with bladder bags and
handtools—but again there was no place to land. Dense forest
was unbroken for miles in all directions, and canoes were already
on the way in. We flew to yet another gravel pit just outside the
wilderness boundary, and hooked up the bucket. John pounded
the black with water drops until an initial attack crew was able to
paddle across Duncan and hike upslope to the fire. The next day
we slung in ten full bladder bags to aid the mop-up.

On June 24 the Squat fire was ready for a final demobilization
of personnel and gear. All but two firefighters had paddled or
flown out earlier, and Steve and I were sent in to manage the
backhaul sling loads, chiefly because they would require hover
hookups in a tight spot.

As John swung 56BH into the final approach, I sucked in a
breath. The helispot was a narrow spit of ledgerock sloping steeply
into deep water on the west side. To the east, a thickly wooded
hillside rose like a bristling rampart. In keeping with light-hand-
on-the-land wilderness tactics, just enough trees had been cut to
safely accommodate (under most conditions) the relatively small
thirty-three-foot rotor blade diameter of the Jet Ranger. As our
skids kissed the rock, I noted that due to the slope, it would be
wise to depart or approach the ship from only the left (downslope)
side; otherwise someone might risk a main rotor "haircut."

John returned to the Seagull helispot, and Steve and I and the
two firefighters spread out a cargo net in the middle of the
ledgerock spit and organized the load—heavy stuff like pumps
and fuel on the bottom, with tents and sleeping bags on top. A

bulky mound of garbage and wet hose ensured two weighty slings, thus two trips for 56BH. Steve and I would take turns with the hookups.

A hover hookup is a potentially hazardous, and therefore glamorous, maneuver that would even pay extra if we were Forest Service employees—25 percent of the base wage, officially called "hazard differential," or more affectionately, "H-pay." It's a gilded bonus for federal grunts that the State of Minnesota doesn't offer, so Steve and I would have to settle for the rush.

I stood beside a bulging net with the swivel raised high in my right hand. Steve was posted behind and to my left, where John could easily see his hand signals from the cockpit of the Jet Ranger. As the helicopter banked and descended in front of me, I saw it settle firmly into the northerly breeze, stabilized in the air flow. As John eased the ship forward and down, aiming for my upthrust arm, I focused on the belly hook protruding from the bottom of the fuselage. I had one foot ahead of the other, bracing against the stiff wind of rotor wash. My goggles were on, my helmet chinstrap secured, foam earplugs in place. The lake surface rippled, glinting waves lapping at the ledgerock ahead of the rotors. There's a bubble of plexiglass at the pilot's feet, and as John dropped in for the top of my head, I glanced up and caught his eye for an instant. Then the skids bracketed my shoulders, and with 56BH holding hover seven feet above the rock, I took a half-step forward and snapped the swivel into the belly hook. I tugged gently ("Don't yank the helicopter out of the sky!" my instructors had admonished) to make sure all was secure, then turned, ducked, and strode quickly away in front of the ship. It was three or four steps to the water's edge, then I angled right through a clump of blueberry bushes to the woods. Steve motioned to John that I was clear, and the Jet Ranger slowly rose, pausing briefly as the lead line stretched full length and the weight of the load (about five hundred pounds) was brought to bear. Then the net was floating over the lake and rising rapidly away toward Seagull.

Steve hooked the second load as I marshaled the ship, and when 56BH returned, Steve and the two firefighters climbed aboard with their personal gear, and I waited on the rock outcrop for the last shuttle.

During the next several minutes I allowed myself to be enveloped by solitude. It was the first time in a week that I had been truly alone, and I suddenly felt disassociated from firefighting. The radio strapped to my chest and the flight helmet cradled in my hands seemed alien. How strange to be on the shore of a Boundary Waters lake, surrounded by wilderness, with no obvious trace of arrival—no wet paddles leaning against an upturned canoe, no trail snaking off into the forest—only a few tree stumps, also alien to this preserve, to hint that I sat on a helispot and had arrived from the sky. I marveled that thirty years had passed since I first traveled in this country, and though I had been a dreamer and an avid spinner of personal fantasies, I never imagined being a firefighter. At age seven I'd even been asked about it. In the small town where I grew up it was well known that one of my uncles was a local firefighter, and one day a second-grade classmate asked me if I was going to be "a fireman" when I grew up. "No," I said, "I'm going to be an artist." By that I meant someone who drew pictures for a living. It sounded cool.

But the future, even when I was much older, had been nebulous at best, and I don't remember any concrete, long-term goals. I did recall that when I first paddled into the BWCAW—at a point barely three miles from where I sat on Squat Lake—the future seemed very near, and of short duration. I did not believe as a teenager that I would live past age twenty-five, and was not at all certain that I desired to. "*I know that I shall meet my fate . . .* " Ah, Yeats—and indeed, that very afternoon Steve and I had come from "*somewhere in the clouds above.*" That sliver of Canadian Shield in the Boundary Waters seemed an ideal spot for a witness post, and I realized that I still was not gazing into the future. The rest of the summer, perhaps the autumn—that was as far as I cared to project a presence. Who knew? I might not survive the afternoon. On our way back to Seagull 56BH could crash through the canopy in a fury of Jet-A flame. Fatalism. It's not a hopeless outlook, but an affirmation of the present. I was, unexpectedly, a firefighter—an airborne firefighter—on a mission, and I relished the privilege. My good fortune christened the day, and I savored the redolent pine and fir; appreciated the rough texture of the rock, warmed by June sunlight; relished the taste of the cooling breeze from over blue water. I had flown into the wilderness, sharing the sky with ravens and eagles, and fate, of course, was free to have her way. At that moment I could conceive of no complaints, "*in balance with this life, this death.*" When 56BH appeared over the treeline, preceded by the distant hum of turbine and rotors, I was ready to go or stay, to live or die—whatever.

I radioed John with a wind report, then slipped on my flight helmet—back on the job.

As we gained altitude, John turned a 360 so I could see all the smokes. To the southeast the Swede and Winchell fires were generating huge, dark columns. To the west we saw a plume from the Topaz fire and a couple of more distant smokes across the border in Ontario. It was evident that no one was going home soon, and John mentioned that we'd been ordered to the burgeoning helibase at the Devil Track Lake airport. We'd been sucked at last into the vortex of the Swede fire—rogue ship no more.

In late afternoon we loaded our personal gear and flew to the airport, joining two other Jet Rangers and their crews. We were assigned motel rooms in the tourist town of Grand Marais, on the shore of Lake Superior.

June 25, 1995

We awoke to dense gray sky and the threat of rain. Four hotshot crews from Idaho and Montana arrived at the Devil Track airport, and our mission was to deliver them and their gear to the wilderness fireground.

Due to my western air operations and helibase experience, I was assigned to be "loadmaster, cargo," in charge of preparing, recording, and shipping all sling loads. It was clear that the Swede and Winchell fires, characterized by remote and rugged terrain, would require a massive aerial supply effort—on the order of five tons of cargo per day. Since the three light helicopters were handling only five hundred to six hundred pounds per load and were also committed to transporting personnel and doing recon flights for the overhead team, it was helpful that we were just past the summer solstice and enjoying a maximum number of daylight hours.

The hotshots were deploying to the bush for an extended stay, so they needed everything, from food and water to pumps and hose. My three-person crew and I quickly filled fourteen nets with about 8,300 pounds of equipment and supplies, and we were confident we had enough time and helicopters to do the job. But at midmorning it started to drizzle, and the ceiling dropped to a few hundred feet. Soon it was pouring, and we scrambled to cover sleeping bags and other sensitive payloads with plastic tarps. All ships were grounded.

We spent the next few hours huddled under rain flies, nursing cups of scalding coffee and trading stories. Over half of the two dozen people assigned to the helibase had flown in from out of state, and I discovered I had friends and colleagues in common with some of them. Ray, the helibase manager, was from the Boise National Forest, and I'd worked for him the previous summer at the Corral Creek fire near McCall, Idaho. He laughed when I reminded him of the day we'd pissed off the US Army, or at least one of their helicopter crew chiefs. Actually, the dude went ballistic.

We were running a hectic early-morning crew shuttle—about one hundred firefighters—out of a meadow in the Payette National Forest. Besides a couple of contract ships, we had a pair of Army Blackhawk helicopters in the loop, and that made us chipper because we could really load them down with people and gear.

We designated one of the Blackhawks as the "tool ship," and when it touched down, flattening the grass with its powerful rotor wash, we formed a human chain to quickly fill it with shovels, Pulaskis, McCleods, and chain saws. As is customary, the handtools were taped in bundles of three and four.

I was at the head of the chain, near the wide doorway of the Blackhawk and directly under the turbine and rotor blades. Despite earplugs, it was almost painfully loud. The military crew chief was in the opposite doorway, arranging the bundles as my partner and I passed them into the helicopter. The chief's flight helmet was linked to the intercom of the ship via a long patch cord that snaked over the ground behind him.

Trying to neatly and systematically stow bundles of mixed handtools, with their variable lengths and protruding tines and blades, is impossible, and I've always been content to quickly stack . such cargo in a safe spot and forget aesthetics. Who cares? But the crew chief, apparently accustomed to tighter, more congenial loads—perhaps all packaged and regimented—was obviously growing irritated with the relative hodge-podge. As I passed him yet another bundle of Pulaskis, I noticed color rising up his neck to his cheeks. As he attempted to wed the Pulaskis to a clutch of McCleods, both bundles shifted and half-rolled to one side, partially entangled with some shovels. The chief exploded.

He threw up his hands and began shouting. I was alarmed for a moment, thinking we had a legitimate, serious problem. I was fascinated to see flecks of saliva spewing from his lips, which I tried to read over the roar of the engine. I thought I picked out a few choice coupled with a wild gesture that clearly referred to the innocent tools. I shrugged and tried to conjure up a sympathetic expression ("hey, I know, I deal with crap like this all the time"), but the chief raged on, looking like a character actor from an overdone scene in a silent movie. When he ripped the microphone out of his flight helmet, I had to turn away. Lord knows, he wouldn't have appreciated my uncontrollable grin. The mike, uprooted, was dangling from his helmet by its wiring. The contrast between his military flight uniform, with its implied professionalism, and his kindergarten behavior was too outrageous.

I glanced toward the cockpit of the Blackhawk and saw the pilot (wearing captain's bars) had sensed a delay and was looking over his shoulder for the crew chief, speaking into his own mike. The chief had spun away from the door, actually stamping his feet. But then he abruptly halted, fumbling with the dangling microphone and attempting to shove it back into place. I surmised the captain was asking him what the hell was happening. I hid my face again, laughing now. The crew chief had shifted his ire from the tools to the hapless avionics system he'd ravaged. Several yards away I could see Ray with a quizzical expression on his face—not unlike the captain.

After another long minute, the crew chief returned from a conference in the cockpit and angrily motioned for me to continue loading. As we finally finished, he walked around the nose of the ship and gestured to his ear. I pulled my plug and bent to his mouth.

"I'm sorry!" he yelled. "That had nothing to do with you!" He smiled sheepishly. I nodded and smiled in return—mainly because his mike, with a stripped screw attached, was still dangling. As I left, Ray approached the chief and spoke to him briefly. Later, I asked him what he'd said. Ray grinned. "I told him that I thought he had a screw loose."

By midafternoon the rain stopped, and the ceiling lifted sufficiently for air operations to resume. A twin-rotor Vertol—84CH (charlie hotel)—belonging to Columbia Helicopters arrived from McCall, Idaho. It was ordered specifically for massive water drops, and came equipped with a one-thousand-gallon bucket.

The Jet Rangers roared to life, and crews were shuttled into the fires, but as sundown approached it became evident that the three light helicopters wouldn't have time to haul a significant portion of my fourteen nets of necessary supplies. We were just beginning to "triage" the loads, tagging absolutely essential drinking water and food items for last-minute runs, when Kevin, the air support group supervisor, hurried over and announced, "I have an idea."

"Wait," I said, "let me guess. We're going to use the Vertol."

"Yup. 84CH can sling these fourteen nets in two big loads."

So my crew and I scampered among the nets with lead lines and swivels, rigging them into a pair of seven-net strings, arranged so that as the Vertol ascended, the slings would lift off the ground one by one, until the seventh net swung 150 feet below the ship.

When we were satisfied that our complicated network of tag lines, swivels, and bull rings was correctly linked, we called for the crew chief of 84CH. He stood amidst the cluster of nets and studied the connections for about ten seconds. Exhaling a drag from his cigarette, he bestowed his imprimatur: "Well, that should work."

"Do you want to hook it?" I asked. It was professional deference. I had worked with a Columbia crew out West once, and they'd been fussy about sling loads and who did what when. Actually I was hoping he'd say "yes" and take control.

"Nah," said the crew chief, dismissively waving his cigarette, "you guys can do it." We had full control, and therefore full responsibility.

So as the Vertol warmed up, we made sure all loose objects on the cargo deck that weighed up to twenty pounds or so were securely stashed under heavier gear, anticipating the tornadolike rotor wash of 84CH. With a hundred feet of longline, we figured the Vertol would be close enough to the ground to whip up a windstorm.

As I stood nearby clutching my radio, 84CH slowly lowered a massive remote hook to the cargo deck, and one of my crew hurried beneath the Vertol to attach the first two-ton load. As the helicopter rose, I held my breath. Not only were these essential supplies, but the entire helibase crew, plus the overhead team at the nearby command post, had dropped what they were doing to watch the show. The longline tightened and the first net lifted off the ground, gently swaying. The lead line dangling from that load stretched taut, and the second net heaved into the air, and so on. I silently counted the slings, and when the seventh left the ground I almost gasped with relief. I hailed 84CH to confirm the destination of that first haul, and then laughed to shed more tension. As the Vertol turned toward the fire, quickly gaining altitude, the seven nets looked like cloves of garlic on a string. The helibase crew was cheering. Despite the weather, the four hotshot crews would be fully supplied by sundown.

June 26–28, 1995

In both memory and brief journal entries, the next three days are a blur of cargo nets and rotor wash. On June 26 we shipped twenty-one sling loads totaling almost ten thousand pounds, including hot dinners at the end of the day, with some of the food pails wrapped in sleeping bags to keep them warm.

Most of the nets were sent out on ten-foot lead lines, so the ships were easing into the cargo deck "low and slow" for hover hookups. Since the Forest Service employees were eligible for hazard pay, and since many wished to stay proficient in the technique, almost everyone eventually migrated over to cargo to perform a couple of hookups. I obligingly inserted them into the rotation, and at one point, during a sudden demand for supplies that coincided with maximum availability of helicopters, we created a fleeting but dramatic rift of aerial choreography.

I was stationed off to one side—radio in hand—overseeing the dance. On my left, beyond a half-dozen full nets, was a line of four helitack people, with a fifth—a marshaller—in a blaze orange vest standing in back of the nets to direct the pilots with hand signals. On my right was a line of four Jet Rangers, hovering twenty-five feet off the tarmac, about a hundred feet apart. The collective music of their turbines and rotors was like a Greek chorus, a ubiquitous background roar for our ongoing air operations narrative, a distinctive melody remembered from fires in Idaho, Montana, Oregon—across the nation and the years, and for some, a poignant hearkening to Vietnam, especially with four ships in an airborne queue.

The first helitacker met the first Jet Ranger at the first load, hooked the swivel, and smoothly bowed away to the pilot's right. As the ship rose gracefully to the left, the next helicopter bumped forward, swinging into the breeze, and the second helitacker sidled to the second net and raised the swivel over her head. They met, touched, and parted. So it unfurled through four evolutions, in romantic clockwork, and the hair rose on the back of my neck.

June 29, 1995

A savvy helibase manager will regularly shuffle people and assignments, or at least offer to. Not only does it bolster morale (especially on a long tour of duty), but it also affords people an opportunity to practice or learn the various skills necessary to run a fireground helicopter operation.

I probably could have remained the "loadmaster, cargo" for the duration, but escaping the visual desert of the airport suddenly seemed attractive, and I volunteered for a three-person heat-hunting mission out on the Topaz fire.

The day before, 55J had flown an infrared recon of the nine-acre burn and detected three lingering hot spots that were not smoking. A crew member equipped with a handheld Xedar camera leaned out the backdoor as the pilot slowly cruised just above the treetops. When the camera revealed a hot spot, another crew member dropped a streamer, a heavy washer with fluorescent pink ribbon attached. It was our job to find those streamers, locate the

associated heat, and extinguish it. The Topaz could then be officially "called out," with no further resources expended.

My two partners were Taiga (his real first name), an experienced, easy-going seasonal from Montana, and Cat, a full-time
Forest Service employee from Ohio. She had drawn a cat's-paw
symbol on the front of her flight suit, and didn't use her last name—
even on the radio. We reported to the seaplane slip on Devil Track
Lake at around 8:00 A.M., then hunkered down for about three
hours, waiting for a low ceiling over the fire to lift and a Beaver to
become available.

As we stacked our gear on the dock, I happened to heft Cat's
fire pack. It was dense as a boulder.

"What the hell have you got in here?" It was a rhetorical question—I didn't really give a damn; she had to carry it—but she
responded by pulling out an item, apparently representative, that
left me incredulous.

"I saw this in a store and couldn't resist," she said, and switched
it on.

It was a battery-operated, two-bladed fan, the size of a small
flashlight. As it whirred away, Cat held it up to her face. "See? Air
conditioning." I shook my head; Taiga snorted.

"Actually," Cat said, now holding the gadget over her head, "I
got it for the helicopter rotor effect—a conversation piece."

"In your fire pack? You're crazy."

She laughed, and I abruptly suspected something, but decided
to wait for confirmation rather than bluntly inquire.

Shortly after noon we heard the throaty rumble of a
DeHavilland Beaver, and a few minutes later it churned around a
point, froth combing over the floats. Several yards from the slip
the pilot cut the engine, and as the propeller jerked to a stop, the
Beaver glided silently up to the dock.

It's an aircraft whose demeanor demands respect and generates
infatuation. It's so ugly it's beautiful—squat and boxy, but radiat-
ing an aura of vigor and durability. The Beaver is thirty feet long,

with a forty-eight-foot wingspan, and despite its businesslike, al-most blunt, appearance, can fly at 115 miles per hour. The slightly bulbous nose and engine cowling, the thick overhead wing, the broad tail that begins its upward slope nearly halfway down the fuselage—lend it the aura of an antique, like a collector's item in air shows rather than a working airplane. It looks like a star of the 1930s, perfect for Indiana Jones or a young Howard Hughes, and the dream ship of hard-core bush pilots.

It was our bus. We laid an upturned seventeen-foot aluminum canoe against the left float, and pilot Dan Ross, a longtime DNR game warden, lashed it to the struts with rope. Taiga and Cat squeezed into the backseat with our packs and Pulaskis, and I clambered into the front. Long, hard use had both polished and tattered the cabin, and as I wiggled through the small doorway, my sleeve snagged a protruding section of weather-stripping and pulled it away from the frame. A tiny brass screw dangled from the strip, and, chagrined, I tried to push it back into its hole with a thumbnail. Ross glanced over and said, "Don't worry about it." So I didn't. After all, I'd been cruising around in a helicopter with doors that popped open in flight.

As we taxied from the dock toward the open lake, I slipped on a set of headphones and studied the console. It was a curious blend of golden-oldie and high-tech. A state-of-the-art programmable radio had been retro-fitted amidst a nest of gauges that might've fit the dashboard of a '51 Chevy. But unlike an old car, the aging Beaver inspired confidence. Here was a time-tested airframe, by god, and the cockpit even smelled righteous—like a well-used, well-oiled baseball glove.

Pilot Ross and I had met at a fire school a few years before, and as we motored through the chop on Devil Track we chatted over the intercom. He was less than a month from retirement, and that initiated a string of anecdotes that would span the entire flight. He swung our nose into the wind and gunned the engine. The sound was solid—part roar, part purr—and resonated in my chest.

Through the soft-focus effect of the whirling prop, I watched the distant treeline sink away as the floats lifted from the waves. We turned northwest, flying just beneath a stratum of scudding gray cumulus.

It was thirty-eight miles and about twenty minutes to Topaz, and it seemed every lake passing by below triggered a fond memory for Ross, who'd patrolled the wilderness for several years. I encouraged his reminiscences, and he responded with relish. I wanted to ask if he was going to miss it, but he mentioned, unbidden, that he was really looking forward to retirement, would be glad to be done with the job. OK. I didn't buy it. There was still too much fire in his eyes and affection in his voice.

The burn encompassed a high knob between Topaz and Amoeber lakes, and we circled it once. The terrain looked mean, and I recalled there had been a medevac of a firefighter who'd fallen and suffered a back injury. Ross tipped the right wing and pointed out the best canoe access—from Amoeber Lake—then banked into the wind and leveled out. Our landing was so smooth that the air and water seemed a single medium, and if I'd punched a stopwatch when I thought our floats split waves, I suspect I would've been at least a second late.

Ross killed the engine, and as the Beaver drifted across the lake, we unlashed the canoe and flopped it into the water. I climbed into the stern, and Cat and Taiga passed down the gear. Then they gingerly eased off the wet float into the Grumman. Ross ordered us to have fun, and I promised we would.

With over six hundred pounds in the canoe we enjoyed only a few inches of freeboard, and I was glad it was less than a quarter-mile to shore. Both of my companions displayed the stiff, gunwale-gripping posture of novices lacking faith in the stability of canoes, and with waves lapping the edges of those gunwales, it was a tense, if short, paddle.

We "beached" the canoe on a flat shelf of rock; then, trading paddles for Pulaskis, we began to slowly grid the burn. Taiga and

I each removed a glove, baring hands to feel for heat in likely spots, and it was then that Cat admitted what I had suspected. I was sure she had little actual fireground experience, but she shocked me by revealing she had exactly none. It was not, however, a sheepish admission. Despite incredulous expressions from Taiga and I, she refused to be embarrassed or apologetic, and just frankly requested guidance in the nuances of hot-spot hunting. She offered no explanation for how she'd managed to become helitack qualified without fire experience, but I figured it was simple chutzpah. So we told her about white ashes, black rocks, hovering insects, and other telltale evidence of latent heat, and how our noses were a valuable tool. We couldn't expect to *see* smoke, so either smell or touch would ferret out our quarry. Cat removed a glove.

We spread out twenty feet apart and inched through the black, raking bare fingers through ash and sniffing the air. Almost immediately Taiga and I caught the faint aroma of smoldering wood—or at least thought we did. An exhaustive search of the surrounding area in a hundred-foot circle produced nothing, but we realized the scent could've drifted downslope from the far side of the burn. After that first fleeting trace of odor we didn't smell it again.

Twenty minutes into the hunt it began to mist, soon thickening to drizzle. We chatted to keep our spirits up.

"So," I said, "'Taiga' is definitely not a nickname?"

"Nope, it's my real name."

"Yeah? Why not 'Tundra'?"

He laughed. "Well, at least you know what 'taiga' means; most people don't. But hey, 'Tundra' is a girl's name."

The drizzle mutated into rain that fell for nearly two hours. We had no choice but to continue our sweeps through the black. Wet rocks were slick under the Vibram soles of our boots, but it was still better to cautiously stalk in the rain than sit in it. Our chatter gradually petered out. There was no trace of pink fluorescent ribbons. The Xedar operator had provided us with a crude map of the burn, drawing three X's where he'd found heat, and we spent extra time in those areas, but saw and felt nothing.

When the rain finally let up, we gathered for lunch at the summit of the knob, to enhance our radio communication with dispatch. I tried to check in, but when I keyed my radio it emitted a weird clicking noise, and I understood that despite my efforts to shield it, moisture had seeped into the electronics.

Encouraged by intermittent shafts of sunlight, I used the screwdriver attachments of my omnipresent Leatherman tool to disassemble the radio and expose the circuit boards. As I gently laid the intricate parts on a flat rock, I realized it might take hours for them to dry unless . . . And, man, I fought the idea—I hate the flavor of crow. But desire for a functional radio outweighed pride.

"OK, Cat," I said, "let me see that damned little fan of yours. I'll use it to dry out my radio."

She howled, gleefully digging into her pack. With a flourish and a smirk she passed me the ridiculous gadget.

"Damn!" I said. "And not a word out of you, Tundra!"

The Beaver wasn't due back until 7:00 P.M.—weather permitting—so we gridded the entire burn again, satisfied it was cold. The waxing sunshine was a tonic, a balm for our disappointment at not finding at least one of the indicated hot spots. We pooled our three estimates of rainfall and reached a consensus at better than a quarter-inch, so any lingering heat was probably quenched anyway, and we'd given that nine acres a thorough cold-trailing—even gazing up into the snags. (A few days later, crews on another fire were finding dead standing birch puffing from their tops like chimneys, where airborne embers had lodged, then smoldered in the punky wood for days.)

At 6:00 A.M. we sat on our upturned canoe, munching the rest of our lunch and admiring a rainbow arching over a wooded palisade across the lake. During the rainfall we'd picked out a potential campsite, expecting to spend the night, and that was not an unpleasant prospect. We had the necessary gear, and it would be a refreshing change from our motel in Grand Marais. But it was also stirring to see the yellow-orange Beaver break into sunlight over Amoeber Lake, emerging suddenly from steel gray skies to the south. The prospect of a pitcher of Guiness Stout at the Harbor Inn wasn't unpleasant either.

As we paddled out to the airplane, nudged by a freshening, pine-scented breeze, Taiga half-turned in the bow, grinning: "And my friends wonder why I love this job?"

June 30–July 3, 1995
In May 1987 there was a fire near Ramshead Lake at the western end of the BWCAW. It wasn't a huge blaze—in the forty-to-sixty-acre range as I recall—but helicopters delivered about fourteen thousand pounds of gear, including thirty thousand feet of hose. When the fire was controlled, the ships were dispatched elsewhere, and firefighters had to abandon the equipment. It sat there for about a month, the wet hose in danger of mildew and rot, and Forest Service officials ultimately decided against the use of helicopters to retrieve it. The emergency was over; thus air operations in the wilderness were prohibited. Instead, the Forest Service called for bids to manually pack out the seven tons, and the resulting tale of struggle, hardship, and bureaucratic fiasco now verges on legend.

I was on the crew of latter-day swashbucklers that carried six miles of hose and other gear out of Ramshead via packframes and canoes, portaging and paddling like seventeenth-century voyageurs—during sweltering June days alive with mosquitoes, flies, ticks, gnats, and trails pounded to quagmires of mud.*

---

*For a full account of this amazing episode, see "The Bizarre and Brutal Ramshead Hose Mission" in *The Bear Guardian* (St. Cloud, MN: North Star Press, 1990).

The mission was so outrageous that I heard about it four months later on a fire in the Siskiyou National Forest in Oregon. When I met a firefighter from California and told him I was from Minnesota, he said, "Yeah? Say, I heard about an incident in the Boundary Waters Wilderness that happened last summer—something about six miles of hose. You know anything?"

I beamed. "Sit down. I'll tell you all about it. I was there."

That's why a colleague approached me one afternoon on the cargo deck at the Devil Track airport, a glint in his eye, and asked, "Hey, have you put in a bid yet?"

"A bid? For what?"

He grinned. "A bid on the job to pack out all the junk we've been shipping into Swede and Winchell."

My laughter was tinged with bitterness. "Oh man! I hope the Forest Service has learned its lesson."

And on June 30 it was clear they had. Word came down from the command post that every effort was to be made by both helitack and fire crews in the bush to backhaul via helicopter any unneeded equipment and supplies as soon as possible. To expedite that order, helitack personnel were flown out to the various helispots to manage the loads and organize people and gear.

For the next four days, I bumped around the fireground from spot to spot by helicopter, canoe, and foot, hustling to keep up with the flow of the operation.

For example, on July 2, 55J flew Steve and me to H-7, a helispot cleared at the crest of ridge above a small, unnamed lake on the Swede fire. I had been at H-7 the day before, helping to pack and hook five nets of tools and garbage. The spot was now clean, but its neighbor—D-6—had a mound of material to be backhauled. But D-6 was too confined and steep for a safe landing, and too thick with dust and ash for hover hookups; all supplies delivered there had arrived at the end of a longline, and that's how they'd have to depart.

Steve and I needed to reach D-6 on the ground, and though it was a bit less than a mile from H-7, a lake and convoluted terrain lay between, and it would be simple to wander astray. So as 55J lifted off H-7, I pulled out my compass and prepared to take a bearing. In less than a minute the Jet Ranger was hovering directly over D-6, and the pilot radioed, "Here we are."

I faced the distant helicopter and sighted along the direction-of-travel arrow of my Silva, then spun the dial to match the magnetic needle.

"Got it, 55J. Thanks." Three hundred forty-five degrees. I gazed along the bearing line and picked out a landmark across the lake— a large birch snag whose white bark contrasted starkly with the green and brown background of singed spruce and fir.

The Jet Ranger banked for the Winchell fire, and Steve and I followed a rocky trail down the ridge from H-7 to the shore of the unnamed lake. Fire crews had cached two canoes at the water's edge, and we dropped our web gear into the bottom of one and shoved off. We paddled west down the narrow lake until we spotted my birch snag, then cut for shore. From the birch I read our course off the compass and we hiked crosscountry through the burn to D-6.

A collection of boulders punctuated a sloping slab of ledgerock, and the place exuded an odor—the garbage was ripening, and it wouldn't take long for the ubiquitous Boundary Waters black bears to catch wind of that. We also had hose, pumps, fuel cans, and miscellaneous gear, and over the next hour we assembled five nets totaling about two thousand pounds.

We notified helibase we were ready to ship, and 56BH made two runs with one hundred feet of longline. The operation was smooth and glitch-free. Then the pilot of 55J came on the air. He was returning to the helibase from his mission on the Winchell fire and decided he might as well "swing in and pick up one of your loads" rather than just dead head all the way home. I instantly replied that it was a longline spot, but he flashed his well-known streak of arrogance: "Oh, I can get in there for a hover hookup," he said.

Yes, we knew. *That* wasn't the point. But it was no time for a radio debate. Besides, 55J was settling on our heads as he spoke. Steve rushed to a net and hoisted the swivel over his head, and I backed off to marshal in the Jet Ranger. Since we couldn't shoot the bastard down, we had to hook him up.

As 55J descended to less than fifty feet, the rotor wash kicked up a storm of ash and dust. By the time the ship's belly hook was within Steve's reach, he and 55J were almost invisible, and my mouth and nostrils were laced with grit. Hand signals were useless, so I talked the pilot in, barely able to see when Steve clasped the swivel home.

"You're clear!" I said, raising my voice over the deafening roar of the turbine engine, magnified in the confines of our little hole in the forest. Steve and I ducked our heads as 55J swirled a tornado of dust and ash in the wake of his rising. The driven, whirling ash penetrated my goggles, causing my eyes to tear. Such particles are also dangerous for helicopter engines.

As soon as 55J cleared the treetops, I called helibase with a pointed message: "D-6 is a longline spot only; I repeat, *longline*." And I bit my tongue to keep from broadcasting, "And send me a rifle."

Next morning was overcast, and serious rain seemed imminent. Reports from the fireground indicated the ceiling was dropping, and the higher ridges would soon be socked in. The long-range forecast favored "cool and wet," and the number-one priority was to pull firefighters, equipment, and garbage off the firelines. Some crews were paddling out—in a fleet of canoes, like a massive Girl Scout expedition—but the twenty-person unit from the Green Mountain National Forest in New England needed to be flown out of H-5, along with nine hundred pounds of gear and three hundred pounds of trash.

Taiga, Cat, and I flew into H-5, on the shore of Lac Lake, with pilot Lee Andrew in 56BH. Using the crew manifest, a document that lists everyone's weight, I quickly broke the crew into five groups of roughly equal poundage, with the heavier of the loads flying last. As 56BH burned off fuel, and hence weight, more payload was allowable.

The sky was perceptibly darkening as we sent off the first four, and their colleagues cracked nervous jokes about being rainbound at H-5, a locale they'd fully experienced. They'd been in the bush for days and were anxious to escape. If foul weather shut down air operations they faced either a long, uncomfortable wait, or a long, miserable hike—all the local canoes were gone. I shared their concern. Since I couldn't leave until all people and cargo were out, I could be stranded too. We held back some tents and food just in case.

By the fourth load, we were splattered by occasional drops of rain, and Lee was reporting smaller gaps between the bottom of the cloud deck and the wooded crests of the high ridges and knobs.

Since Taiga was slated for demob that evening, we put him on the fifth load. Then Cat and I and the assistant crew boss of Green Mountain rushed to rig three net loads of gear and garbage, and Lee slung them out in two trips—we hooked a pair of lighter nets together.

We, the last three off H-5, gratefully climbed aboard for the eighth shuttle. With rain streaking the plexiglass, some of the high knobs were already wreathed in cloud. As we leveled off for the airport, Lee keyed the intercom and said, "Well, I think we just made twenty people very happy."

"Affirmative," I replied, "and you know Lee, a lot of folks go through their whole lives without making twenty people happy."

July 4, 1995
Independence Day, and 56BH was released from the fires, along with John the pilot and the original "rogue ship" crew from the

Devilfish fire—Dean, Steve, and myself. We were cleared to fly to Grand Rapids, with a stop at Side Lake for me, but at 8:00 A.M. the ceiling was too low to lift off the airport.

I share a particular mindset with many wildland firefighters: you can't wait to be dispatched to a fire, and during the operation you wish only for more hours and more action, but once overhead says you're officially demobilized, you can't wait to leave. In part, of course, because leaving will automatically make you available for the next dispatch.

By midmorning we were champing at the bit, and John figured that if we flew inland for Ely, further away from the influence of fogbound Lake Superior, we might encounter a higher, more trustworthy ceiling. He suggested that as soon as we could slip out of the airport we should do so, taking our chances with the skies of the BWCAW one more time. It was agreed, and around eleven that morning we shook hands with the two helicopter crews remaining. "We'll see you in five minutes," said Ray, assuring us that we'd be forced to turn back when we smacked into a solid cloud bank over the first ridgeline. We took off, believing he might be right.

It was close. At one point John had to take us down to nearly treetop level to dodge the hanging rim of overcast, but he was vindicated—the closer we got to Ely, the lighter and higher the cloud deck became, and we landed there to check the weather computer. Things looked dandy all the way to Grand Rapids, and Side Lake was almost directly on the flight path. We chatted briefly with a Northwest Airlines flight crew out on the tarmac, comparing weather notes.

Back in the air, Dean radioed Superior National Forest dispatch in Grand Rapids and requested that they phone my wife, Pam, and inform her that we'd be landing at the baseball field in Side Lake. John had asked me, "Where's your house? I'll set down in the yard." But I told him that we didn't, unfortunately, have the necessary rotor clearance, and besides, we'd scare hell out of the dog.

Several minutes later, as the Side Lake fire tower came into view on the horizon, it occurred to me that it was the Fourth of July and the ball field might be crawling with kids. I thought about a local gravel pit as an alternative, but the cool, cloudy weather was an ally. The field was deserted, and I pointed out the power lines to John.

The skids of 56BH creased the infield grass between second and third base—a short stop in more ways than one—and I hopped out of the backseat. I grabbed my pack out of the cargo bay, shook hands all around, then checked the sky for John and flashed a thumbs-up.

Before the rotor song died away in the distance, I was hiking for the road with my red pack on my back. Up to that very moment I'd been on the payroll. What a country.

August 10, 1995

I met Pam on the highway. She was on her way home from work, and I flashed my headlights. I pulled my truck onto the shoulder and she U-turned and parked behind me. Her expression was savvy—she'd seen my yellow Nomex shirt. I was leaving again.

As we embraced she asked the Three Questions: Where? (Back to the Gunflint.) What? (Not helitack this time; I'd be an engine boss on an engine strike team.) The last query, though she knew the answer, had to be raised—how long? (Open-ended; what else? Probably no more than twenty-one days, but could be shorter; I'd certainly been out longer.) My allegiance to a personal credo concerning wildfire—"anytime, anywhere"—had wedged between us before. Pam was disappointed but accepting.

Six hours later I was nestled into a sleeping bag on the floor of a church basement (carpeted) in Grand Marais, with the other nine members of our strike team—all DNR smoke chasers. We had two one-ton wildland engines, a minivan utility vehicle, and most important, a mission.

The cause of our mobilization was the Sag Corridor fire, an explosive blaze that had burned over a thousand acres in a few blustery hours, ripping into Ontario from an escaped campfire in the BWCAW near Romance Lake. (A ten-thousand-dollar reward would soon be posted for information leading to the arrest, etc. Uncle Smokey was not happy.) However, we weren't a part of the Sag Corridor operation. We had the good fortune to be assigned to the local Forest Service district as an initial attack crew for the new fires that were expected to break out. One already had, and our boats would be ready in the morning.

August 11–12, 1995
We drove to a resort on Clearwater Lake, about a mile and a half south of the Canadian border, and stowed our engines in the parking lot. We were now an amphibious force, and the first boat—a fourteen-foot Lund aluminum with a ten-horse outboard—was waiting at the dock. Clearwater is a motorized Boundary Waters lake, long and narrow, deep and blue-green, rimmed with magnificent rock escarpments—like a Norwegian fjord. The fire, ignited by lightning, had torched about three acres. It was located five miles down the lake, and the forty-minute cruise seemed like a river trip. I studied the map, ticking off designated campsites as landmarks, periodically looking behind to establish a fix on how the cliffs would appear on the way back. The fire and the boats were being turned over to us.

When the prow scraped rocks at the portage from Clearwater to Mountain Lake, I inhaled the pungent perfume of smoldering balsam fir—the sweetest of all wood smokes, and for me an incense so potent that it's a mood-altering drug. Even in the dead of winter, a whiff of fir smoke thrills my spirit with vivid impressions of heat, flame, and May, spurring fond memories and great expectations, conjuring the sooty faces of comrades.

That morning the burning balsam aroma was like a hearty breakfast and a fresh cup of coffee. I was ready to work. I snuggled into my web gear and pack, and being the first of our crew on the scene, assigned myself to scout the fireground. One of the firefighters who'd been there all night guided me in.

We hiked up the portage trail until an orange ribbon tied to a pine limb pointed us east into the woods. We followed a hoselay until we hit the Border Route backpack trail, which steered us directly into the black. The fireground straddled the trail.

A familiar voice hailed me. It was Mark Adams, ubiquitous Stihl chain saw in hand, and we chuckled through our greetings, appreciative of the symmetry between this meeting and our role reversal from the Devilfish encounter; I was now relieving him. He briefed me on the fire and the terrain—the latter being steep, bouldery, and treacherous, with a sheer drop at one spot—and as we parted we exchanged the same benediction we had a month before: "See you at the next one."

When our crew was assembled, we spread out in three teams, wielding Pulaskis and one-inch hoselines to flush out the heat. Adams and the initial attack squad had cut a rough line around the fire and secured the edges, but inside that perimeter virtually every square yard of ground was hot—duff, root wads, deadfalls, snags, and baked rocks that we dare not touch with a bare hand.

Knowing it would be a long, arduous day, I purposely settled into the rhythm of mop-up, methodically bumping from smoke to smoke, counting small victories, and soothed by the music of the fireground: the thudding and clinking of Pulaskis on rock and wood; the hiss and whoosh of cold water transformed to steam; the laughter, grunts, and curses of my colleagues; and finally, when weariness needed to be held at bay, my own soft singing, the lyrics and melodies engendering a low-key joy that eased pain and greased the clock.

The work was drudgery. Like most mop-up it was tedious, difficult, and dirty. When I first had seen the burn I had lost the edge of excitement, acutely aware of how grueling the next ten hours would be. I had grimaced at Adams, saying, "What a lousy spot to take a boat ride to."

Nevertheless, by the end of the shift I was happy, verging on euphoric. I know a large share of the credit lies with certain protein molecules produced in my body that cause analgesic and mood-elevating effects in response to prolonged exertion. If endorphins did not exist, the Forest Service would have to invent them for issue in pill form. But for me there is also an intellectual response—the sure knowledge of vocation, the utter conviction that firefighting is something I was born to do. I've discovered a niche where I snugly fit like a hose coupling onto threads.

So yes, the benevolent biochemicals vaccinate me against the disease of morose fatigue, but my mind acknowledges the love of accomplishment and the nobility of the toil. There is poetry in sweat. We are built to struggle, and quickly wither in the absence of challenge, even if that challenge is merely to sing in the face of weariness and pain.

By sunset no visible smokes remained, but none of us entertained the illusion that we'd nailed them all. Still, it was pointless to babysit the scene overnight, so we clambered into the boats and cruised back to the resort, awed by the sun-stained smoke column from the Sag fire.

We drove down the Gunflint Trail to Okontoe, and I claimed the same bunk I'd slept in six weeks earlier, then enjoyed a noisy reunion with the kitchen staff. The place was evolving into a second home.

Next morning we reported to the ICP at the Seagull Guard Station, and I bumped into Tom Schackman and Steve Jakala. Handshakes and grins—yes, the circle is small and we all seem to show up at fires like moths to a candle—or flies to fresh dung—drawn into a powerful symbiotic relationship with our unpredictable trade.

I volunteered to take five people back out to the Clearwater fire and finish it off. My guess was that we'd find at least twenty hot spots, and we decided to count. We lined out and performed three slow grids of the burn, everybody with one glove off, meticulously checking every square yard. On the first pass we killed eleven—with only a couple actually showing smoke. On the second grid, reversing direction for fresh perspective, we found four, and the last time through, one. The burn was cold, and I saw no reason we shouldn't pull all the hose (about a thousand feet) and pile it into our boats.

While we were packing watermelons of wet, dirty hose down the portage trail, we encountered two parties of campers carrying their canoes and gear up the trail to Mountain Lake and the Ontario border, and I like to think we added a certain *je ne sais quois* to their wilderness experience. Perhaps we merely startled them.

One group was all female, a woman and four young girls, and one—she looked about ten years old—was having a wretched tussle with a seventeen-foot aluminum canoe. She was puffing and suffering (and griping), and one of my firefighters said he was going to stop and help her on his way back for more hose. I talked him out of it.

"You'll ruin her portage, man." I argued. "She's hurting now, but she'll be proud at the end. Don't rob her of a good story, a good challenge. Would you want someone to do your mop-up for you?"

"Damn right!" he said, but grinned and left the girl to her burden.

August 13, 1995
We spent the morning at a Forest Service boat landing on Seagull Lake, repairing a dock, reinforcing a section of rock riprap, and generally sprucing up the facility. Given the dry weather, it seemed

merely a matter of time before we'd be needed on a new fire, but meanwhile the local folks employed us to catch up on maintenance chores.

In early afternoon our two engines and a third Forest Service rig reported to a gravel pit a few miles south of the ICP. A Sikorsky S-64 Skycrane helicopter, one of the largest ships in the world, was slated to use the pit as a helispot in about three hours, and we needed to prepare it. First we spread out on foot and picked up all loose objects—branches, cones, litter—anything that the seventy-five-foot rotor blades of the Skycrane would turn into missiles by generating a tornado when it landed. Next we unreeled hose from the engines and attempted dust abatement. The gravel pit was like a desert, and the first splash of the 200 gallons in my engine seemed to vanish before the last spray hit the ground. The three engines dumped three loads apiece—about 1,800 gallons—shuttling water from a nearby creek. The sand looked damp, but it wasn't wet enough. When the Skycrane, rotors flared, began to settle in, a vicious dust storm twisted out of the pit, almost obscuring the gigantic, ten-ton helicopter. The pilot opted not to land, and was forced to return to the Grand Marais airport. Since the folks on the Sag Corridor fire were keenly anticipating the massive water drops of the Skycrane (it can sling a two-thousand-gallon bucket), finding a base for it in the neighborhood was a priority. We heard that a better spot was found next day, the only caveat being an abandoned septic tank that had to be towed off the site—dung abatement.

But we were otherwise engaged.

August 14, 1995

As I survey my journal I find that for the past seven years, I've been working fire duty somewhere—Idaho, Oregon, Minnesota—on August 14. As lush summer foliage begins to dry and lightning-rich thunderstorms pound the land, long August afternoons—already baked in the sun—are glorified by sudden bursts of fire. Via a combination of persistence and luck, I've either been in the right place at the right time or been quickly shipped there. On this August 14 my luck was golden.

Our morning at Okontoe was routine—coffee, breakfast, turns in the deluxe, double-stall outhouse, and a phone call from headquarters in Grand Marais with our orders for the day. There was an old helispot on a ridge near Clearwater Lake that required rehabilitation.

We drove down a dead-end logging road and found it—an "X" formed by concrete paving tiles in an overgrown meadow. With brush cutters and a chain saw we refurbished it. Despite the racket (or perhaps drawn by it) a pair of regal whitetail bucks—one with at least ten points—minced across the middle of the opening, pausing/posing for several seconds to stare at us. Inevitably, someone yanked a plastic camera out of a fire pack and snapped a few photos, probably wondering much later what the hell those two brown dots were supposed to be.

In general terms, these fires were good for the deer, eventually generating more food and habitat. And in specific terms these fires were good for my colleagues and me, generating paychecks for more groceries and mortgage payments. We were one with the whitetails.

By noon the helispot project was complete, and our minivan and four people were sent to the Grand Marais airport to reinforce another strike team. Our two one-ton engines with three of us in each, were directed to report to the mid-Trail area near Poplar Lake and stand by there for the afternoon.

We found a shady bower on a side road that was out of sight but close to the highway—an ideal place to hunker down. We set our radios to "scan" and settled into the grass with our lunches and a newspaper. I had just begun the crossword puzzle when we heard an aerial observer report a new fire, " . . . just north of Poplar Lake."

Six heads jerked up and froze. An instant later we were scrambling into our engines, remains of lunches thrown on the floor, newspaper sections crammed behind the seats. Poplar Lake! Us!

When the observer broadcast the legal description, we realized we were about a half-mile from the fire. The radio traffic was urgent. The fire was cooking through an aspen cutover and surging toward structures on the Gunflint Trail. This was Overhead's nightmare scenario come true: a second major fire cuts the Trail, destroying buildings and forcing a mass evacuation, knocking out the main power line, and compromising suppression operations on the Sag Corridor. Disaster. This Poplar Lake fire had to be hit hard—quenched with extreme prejudice, *now*—and we owned the closest engines.

But how to get there? We scanned our maps and compared them to the surroundings. So near and yet so far. There were three narrow, two-track roads in the Poplar Lake vicinity that left the Gunflint heading north toward the fire. We glimpsed occasional puffs and wisps of smoke, but our best indicator was the four-engine air tanker that appeared overhead. In a stroke of luck, the loaded tanker—bound for the Sag incident—was practically on top of Poplar Lake when the fire turned up. The tanker was diverted immediately, and began to drop retardant on the blaze. Two Beavers were also enroute.

Our strike team leader, Forest Service regular Tom McCann, was racing down the Trail from Seagull with two more engines, and a Minnesota DNR conservation officer was already on the highway in front of us. We pulled over to the shoulder across from Windigo Lodge. The best tactic was to wait for more information. It would be a mistake to commit ourselves to the wrong route. But an elderly woman, frantic with fear, rushed out yelling. What she saw was two fire engines and six firefighters doing nothing—with a column of smoke in the background.

"It's up that road!" She pointed at one of the narrow logging roads.

"That will take us to the cutover?"

"Yes! Yes! Why are you just standing here?"

The woman was distraught. Windigo Lodge had burned down a couple of winters before, killing several guests. I tried to explain that we were waiting for our aerial observer to determine the best way in, but she wouldn't hear it. I knew I should wait, but her loud, insistent plea was convincing. I hesitated, then rationalized: she's a local, she ought to know the country, right? I caved in to her panic. With the CO's pickup in the lead (investigating officers were being dispatched with initial attack crews to begin searching for a cause immediately), we locked in the hubs, then bounced and weaved down a dusty, two-track trail that grew increasingly more rugged as we penetrated the forest. About a quarter-mile in we encountered a stretch of boulder patch that looked impassable. The CO and I rushed ahead on foot for a hundred yards, and it only got worse. By this time McCann and his two engines were behind us, and the lead plane for the air tanker was overhead. Air Attack radioed that he saw our caravan, and that access to the fire was on a different road, one about a quarter-mile to a half-mile further west on the Gunflint. So much for the expertise of the locals. The CO flashed a crooked grin, our better judgement had been clouded by someone else's fear.

We backed into the brush to get our engines turned around, and now McCann, who was last in, was first out and thus in the lead. I cheerfully cursed, rueful that we'd been "demoted" from first-engine-in to last by a simple change of venue.

We hit the highway and hung a right, light bars blazing. The asphalt was exhilarating, like paddling fast, deep water after dragging through mud flats. A couple hundred yards down the road we sped past another narrow trail, half-concealed by foliage, and one of my firefighters said, "Did you see that? I wonder if that's it?"

A moment later Air Attack called McCann and told him we'd just blown by our turnoff. Five sets of brake lights glowed, as if automatically triggered by the voice of Air Attack. As I executed a

"Y" turn in the middle of the highway, my partners and I laughed. We had the lead back, first-engine-in.

The logging trail was rocky and rutted, and a huge aspen deadfall blocked the way. I could see at least two other trees across the road further on. I told one of my crew to break out the chain saw, and heard McCann spreading that word as he hiked up from the rear of our stalled column.

"There's probably a lot of this blowdown," he said to me. "You and I'll head to the fire on foot and do a size-up."

I slung on my web gear, and after McCann and I vaulted over the deadfall, I took a long draught from a canteen to help prepare for battle. A firefighter runs on water.

The cramped, partially overgrown road seemed like a tunnel through the forest, but the sensation of constriction and confinement was due less to the actual width of the trail than to my acute awareness that we were striding amidst a massive concentration of fuel. And we had not yet seen the fire nor judged the actual strength of our enemy. We were the point of the strike team, plunging forward toward the unknown, and I was high on undiluted joy. To savor such moments is reason to breathe.

The roar of the air tanker's final pass resounded through the trees, and McCann got on the radio. By this time, what was known as the Poplar Lake fire was priority one. The entire Superior National Forest was listening intently, realizing this was a critical incident. Literally hundreds of our peers—from the Sag ICP to the big dogs at MIFC in Grand Rapids—were staring at their radios, waiting for a report from the ground. Air Attack had relayed what he could see through smoke from above, but aerial scouting, though extremely helpful, is rarely definitive and sometimes misleading. We "ground pounders" needed to get there.

McCann keyed his mike and hailed Grand Marais dispatch. He told them about the blocked road, then said, "Pete Leschak and I are hiking in to do the size-up."

I could've hugged him. He didn't have to mention my name. *He* was the strike team leader, and a terse message saying that *he* was heading in to the fire was all that was required or expected. Given the situation, I understood that with that single broadcast sentence he did more for my reputation and career than I could accomplish with a season's work. That is, if we effectively handled the Poplar Lake fire. Being prominently identified with a fire attack gone sour might be a durable, permanent association. In the fire service there *is* such a thing as bad publicity.

A few hundred yards from the fire we saw a small kettle lake only three or four chains west of the trail, and McCann pointed. "Potential water source," he said. He had a portable pump on his engine, and between the four rigs we carried over a thousand feet of inch-and-a-half hose, and could have more delivered in a matter of minutes.

The smoke thickened, and suddenly we were slogging through grass and brush dripping red with fire retardant. The tanker pilot had expertly laid one of his drops directly on the old logging road, and it would serve as our initial control line.

The fire was loud—snapping, crackling, and occasionally roaring as pockets of lighter fuel exploded. The empty air tanker had departed, but two Beavers were making rapid sorties, thundering in just above the treetops to dump their two-hundred-gallon loads in shimmering swaths.

McCann and I split up to scout the perimeter of the fire, and I steered around the west flank, pacing off the distance in chains— or at least attempting to. The fire was burning in aspen slash and regeneration, fringed by mixed fir and birch, and given the stumps and deadfalls, the footing was difficult. I tallied a few chains, then estimated the rest. I pegged the blackened area at three to four acres, or a bit less, and now growing relatively slowly. The air tanker had painted lines all the way around the fire, and the retardant was effectively hindering the blaze for the moment. But there was plenty of fresh fuel beyond the slurry lines, and I was surprised to note how vigorously the thick green aspen regeneration had burned, then carried fire up into mature timber.

Between Beaver sorties I cut through the black, and the ovenlike heat was almost overpowering—like being in a two-hundred-plus-degree dry sauna. The heavier residue of the logging operation ensured a tough mop-up job, supporting hundreds of strongholds of stubborn heat. But we still had running fire to kill before we worried much about that, and when I tied in with McCann we quickly agreed on a plan. A bulldozer had been dispatched automatically and would soon be on scene. He ordered a second dozer, and I suggested we request a medium helicopter from the Sag fire to provide us with bucket drops in the heavy fuels. At least one Beaver would stay. Once our four engines arrived we'd deploy along the trail, knock down the flames pushing against the slurry line, then start working around the perimeter until the bulldozers could contain it. By then we should have an ample and reliable water supply established from the kettle lake, and we'd ring the burn with a hoselay and drown it.

The CO joined us as we made another survey of the scene. "What's it look like?" he asked. "Are we going to stop this one?"

To appreciate McCann's reply you should understand that fire fighting is a relatively small part of his life. What the Forest Service usually requires of him revolves around a desk and a computer, and his true passion is art. He's a painter, and even as we sucked smoke near Portage Lake, his accomplished work was on display at a special exhibition in Grand Marais, featuring a series of sensitive landscapes done in the Ontario village of Rossport and entitled "Clothed In The Sun." His speech and demeanor are gentle and patient, and there is little hint of the stereotypical machismo that one learns to expect from an ex-Marine like McCann. Except, apparently, in the heat and lather of initial attack.

For when the CO asked us, "Are we going to stop this one?" McCann's alert but placid features temporarily collapsed into the wicked scowl of a drill sergeant. He clenched a fist and growled, "We're going to kick its ass!"

I would like to have captured him on film at that moment— face streaked with sweat and soot, capped by a helmet and grimacing like a berserker in a bayonet drill. The enlarged print could be exhibited with his paintings and titled "Clothed In Nomex." I've long been fond of the notion of an "artist/warrior" or the "soldier/poet." (More on that later.)

I was pleased with McCann's confident enthusiasm. Number one on the list of Standard Fire Orders is "Fight fire aggressively, but provide for safety first." Our scouting mission and the heavy air support were our safety net, and now we were going to be aggressive.

Our caravan of engines emerged from a screen of trees with mine in the lead, and McCann and I lined them out along the active north flank, slowly backing them in so they could escape more quickly if need be. When mine was in position anchoring the northeast quadrant of the fire, we deployed our hoseline and charged it with a mixture of water and Class A fire-fighting foam, directly attacking the flames.

Foam is a surfactant that breaks down the surface tension of water, allowing greater penetration into fuels, thus effectively stretching water supply. Also, by adjustment of the ratio of foam concentrate to water, bright white blankets and piles of heat-reflecting bubbles can be laid on fuels, hence slowing or stopping the spread of fire. Soon the flank was dotted with spumescent patches and windrows of foam, and steam swirled with smoke where two-to-four-foot flames had been snapping only minutes before.

Soon all four engine crews were strung out on the flank, working the line with hoses and pump cans. The turnaround time for the two Beavers was so short that it seemed we were pelted with a drumfire of water drops. As one of the planes roared in from the west, I'd turn away and take the cold spray of the load on my

back. It was a welcome shower. The heat was stifling, and to remain in one place for more than a minute or two was to risk a
singed boot and foot. We took care to snake our hoselines over
wet ground or cool logs. It's tacky to fry hose.

The first bulldozer clattered up and began gouging out a line
in the northwest corner of the fire, pushing south. A BIA engine
followed it in, dowsing the line. Our medium helicopter appeared
overhead, a Bell 212 with a fixed belly-tank and snorkel instead of
a bucket; it looked like a three-hundred-gallon load. McCann
directed the ship to the south flank ahead of the dozer, and the
drops had immediate, significant effect. In less than a half hour
after our engines reached the fireground, we were clearly into the
mop-up stage. A local volunteer fire department set up a large
portable tank, and our people kept it full with a Mark-III pump
set up at the kettle lake. Our engines refilled from the tank.

As it happened, my friend Catherine, a reporter for Minnesota
Public Radio, was at the Sag fire that day, preparing a story. She
left the area before the Poplar Lake fire broke out, and later in the
afternoon when she inquired about any new developments, Overhead informed her of the new fire start and said that we had
"stomped on it." No lie. The warrior in artist McCann kept his
vow. There was not a type of suppression resource available to us
that we did not employ—aggressively.

By late afternoon the dozer line was complete, all running fire
was out, and all air support had been released—the two Beavers
to a new fire. McCann had also been dispatched there, and Tim
Norman, the fire management officer of the Gunflint District,
brought us sandwiches and cold drinks. He appointed Vern
Northrup, the BIA engine boss, as the new IC, and told us to
work the fire until we felt it was safe to leave.

Using gated wyes and one-inch hose, we gradually extended a
network of attack lines and nozzles over the entire fireground.
The strike team split up into several two- and three-person teams,

and by dusk the sound and fury of the early afternoon settled down to quiet and painstaking mop-up. At 9:00 P.M. we were picking our way in the narrow glare of headlamps, periodically switching them off to search for shining orange embers or to admire the glittering starscape overhead.

At around ten o'clock, I noticed a tangerine glow in the east and nudged my partner. "Let's take a break."

We sat on warm boulders and watched the moon rise out of the forest canopy. The gibbous disk was only three days past full, and the burgeoning lunar lamp, flattened and magnified near the horizon, slowly brightened from the tone of dull embers to a brilliant silver, illuminating the fireground and surrounding woods. Isolated birches stood out as pillars of ice or ghostly candles of white flame. The dozer line cut through the hazel brush and aspen saplings like a chalky river of dust, appearing almost natural in forgiving moonlight. Our serpentine hoselays looked like branching veins and arteries on the surface of a black heart.

If not for the sudden chill—we were soaked with sweat and water—it would've been difficult to get moving again. But by then the beauty was pervasive, with moonglow painting our world in celestial maquillage. It was easy to labor in such light, and besides, we were nearing the finish. The Portage Lake fire was cold enough to sleep.

By midnight we were wolfing down supper at Okontoe. Our hosts had stayed up late, keeping food warm, and we were effusively grateful. A contingent of Overhead arrived from Grand Marais with congratulations (and assignments for the morning), and we felt prosperous.

We are expendable because we are warriors. It's not that we're sacrificial victims or cannon fodder, like human bridges across barbed wire in the horror of a World War I battlefield. We are more coddled than that. Rather, it's because we know the joy of forgetting, the altered state of mind that comfortably ignores the self; and that which is forgotten or ignored is expendable.

The British soldier-poet Wilfred Owen, while immersed in the mindless brutality of trench warfare in 1918, produced what is arguably the most potent and wrenching (and beautiful) anti-war poetry ever written. Yet he also won the Military Cross for heroism in combat, and in a letter home he wrote about the particular battle where he "lost all earthly faculties, and fought like an angel."

On fire, I have been there. I do not place myself and my comrades in a league with Owen, for as he wrote of his fellow soldiers, "Weep, you may weep, for you may touch them not." But I know how to fight like an angel. At Poplar Lake, and hundreds of other blazes, I traversed the fireground like a disembodied spirit, focused only on the struggle, on the flow of the attack, on the heady geometry of tactics and logistics, and on the faces of my firefighters.

Were we in danger? Yes. Could we have been injured or killed? Yes. Did we care? No. In *The Art of War*, Sun-tzu quotes *The Book of Changes, the I ching:* "In happiness at overcoming difficulties, people forget the danger of death." In the tumult of initial attack you are outside the self. Fear and courage are irrelevant. There is no pain nor apprehension of disaster; for a time, at least, there is only joy and vitality.

As I write this, the U.S. Congress is debating President Clinton's decision to send American troops to the former Yugoslavia. In the midst of the argument, a congressman held up a copy of *Time* magazine. The cover showed a U.S. solider, and the headline read: "Is Bosnia Worth Dying For?" The congressman thought not.

But of course, in the context of a military operation, the question is bogus, a political ploy. To the soldier, the real question is, is being a warrior in the armed forces of the United States worth dying for? He or she has little choice concerning where or what, specifically, to die for. Clinton might have phrased the question, "Is an attempt at securing peace in the long-suffering Balkans, the traditional powder keg of Europe, worth dying for?"

In July 1994, fourteen of my fellow firefighters died on a fire in Colorado. *Time* magazine could have produced a cover that asked: Was Storm King Mountain worth dying for? or, more explicitly, were the stands of Gambel oak and pinyon-juniper brush worth dying for? Negative. No one there intended to be burned to death on their behalf.

But like soldiers, we are expendable. We stand between society and a perceived menace, and it is implicitly understood that there will be casualties. Society doesn't expect to lose car dealers, beauticians, or Wal-mart greeters in the line of duty, but a certain number of firefighters are disposable. And just as soldiers don't serve for the sake of Bosnia (or Kuwait, or South Vietnam), we don't risk our health and safety for vegetation, or even for buildings. We do it for the joy, and to temporarily abandon the self and fight like angels.

We are privileged.

After the Poplar Lake fire, for most of three days, our engine strike team cleaned and stained outhouses at campgrounds and trailheads. On the surface, onerous labor—unglamorous, tedious, malodorous. But not unchallenging, at least for those who realize that through practice a warrior learns patience. Through placid waiting, you learn how to fight. Our shining fire engines stood quiet in the sun, haulers of rags, paint thinner, brushes, and brooms. Reality check.

The morale of some greenhorns began to suffer, but for me it was thus: the privies did need attention; it might as well be ours. Commit to it. Doing a good job is easier than hurried, slipshod work, even if it's only the rehabilitation of an outhouse. Self-discipline is about striving for quality when the stakes are low. Anyone can be galvanized on initial attack, but responsibility and will are truly tested by the grind of everyday life.

We are privileged because after the elation of dancing with smoke and flame, it's easier for us to see the difference between the courage required by combat and the more needful, more refined courage required by all who desire to lead a decent life. Integrity, fairness, respect—and worthy outhouses—are more precious than glory. Anyone can fight like an angel.

CHAPTER TWELVE

The Fire Triangle

The boundaries which divide Life from Death are at best
shadowy and vague. Who shall say where the one ends,
and where the other begins?

Edgar Allan Poe

Helicopter Nine-Five-Whiskey banked out of swirling smoke and leveled out forty feet over the bog. I saw the rotor disk stabilize in the airflow, like a whirling gear clutched to a shaft. A red fifty-five-gallon drum of napalm dangled beneath the Jet Ranger, cradled in the cables of a helitorch.

The ship accelerated, aiming for us, and in a moment flaming globs of alumagel spewed from the torch, arcing aft and plopping into mats of leatherleaf and tall grass. Bursts of flame quickly merged into a wave of fire surging north across the bog.

I was perched on a J-7 Bombardier, a tracked vehicle designed to tread and "float" across waterlogged ground. We were "wet-tracking" the southern control line of a 1,343-acre prescribed burn in northeastern Minnesota, our treads imprinting a pair of shallow, water-filled ruts to prevent the fire from escaping its assigned bounds. Carlisle pushed the J-7 to top-end, lurching eastward over hummocks, rocking like a skiff in rollers.

In seconds the helicopter closed in from 250 yards behind, its spoor an instant train of fire, as if pursued by implacable burning zombies clawing at the sky. Through reflected clouds in the plexiglass bubble of the ship I saw the pilot. The burgeoning fire was linked to his right thumb pressing the control button of the helitorch.

He bored in as if to attack, as if to meld us with the napalm haze and the blackening biome. Closer, closer—and we whooped to see the torch swaying between the skids, and our terrific fire quickening into an orange tide. Fifty yards . . . forty . . . thirty . . . then the pilot killed the torch and broke away to the north, vanishing into smoke.

The J-7 churned on, flinging cold water from the treads, and in two minutes Nine-Five-Whiskey reappeared behind, locked in and chasing us with fire. We repeated the dangerous dance four times, until our hot line was a mile long and our smoke column like a pinnacle of cumulus. We laughed and hollered and Lightfoot exclaimed, "That's the way it's supposed to be done!"

I was charged with elation.

Six days before, I was prostrate on an examining table, focused on the sweep second hand of a wall clock, bemused by the banality of cowardice. As fretful minutes snaked by I engaged the "if only" fantasy.

If only I'd skipped that routine fire department physical the previous month—as several of my colleagues did. It was a biennial screening: Are you fit enough to don a SCBA (self-contained breathing apparatus) and mount an internal attack on a structure fire? That is, are you healthy enough to be abused by overexertion and extreme stress? Fit enough to expose yourself to some of the most hazardous environments on the planet?

And *if only* a urinalysis hadn't been part of the screening—never was before. Because then I'd be blissfully unaware of the traces of blood in my urine.

I felt fine. No, I felt great; mustered only symptoms of wellness. But now I knew of red blood cells in my pee. The report stated I should certainly consult my physician. I did.

He was jovial at first—ordered another urine test, expressing confidence that the cells were a transitory phenomenon and fresh results would be negative. He left the room to fetch the report and returned in a few minutes. My doctor was no longer jolly. As he entered he said, "Rats!"—like he'd just muffed an easy putt. It was chilling. "Rats!"

He pulled no punches. "Still might be nothing," he said, "but it could be cancer." Strangely, that didn't sound as bad as "rats!" Bottom line: more tests.

The C-word was a lightning bolt, but after a stab of fear I settled into a workaday dread of the tests themselves. *Cancer* was too abstract, too outrageous. I couldn't stay excited about that. I wasn't frightened by what the tests might reveal as much as I was by the procedures themselves: they all required needles. I hate them; they set me quivering. I'm so phobic about needles that when I have a tooth filled I eschew Novocain. Better the drill than the needle. Any day. I make my dentist very nervous.

So I gazed at the wall clock second hand—at time made visible—trying for a focus beyond the shame of my fear. A nurse approached with a needle.

The test was an IVP (intravenous pyelography), and the sturdy hypodermic was to inject a viscous, radiopaque dye into my bloodstream and thence to my kidneys and urinary tract. A series of X-rays would ensue. I'd prepped myself with a prescribed regimen of laxatives and a fast.

Barbara brandished the needle (I appreciate name tags as well as clocks), and I silently said, *relax*. I was aware of her jab but felt only the slightest of pricks. She was good! Aloud I said, "You're good with a needle," hoping I didn't sound giddy.

"Thanks," she replied, in a professional monotone. I was disappointed she didn't seem more flattered. Beneath the flimsy paper gown I felt a rime of sweat at the waistband of my underwear.

"Don't move," Barbara said. I obeyed, captive to the needle. She pumped the syringe for a long time. Then, alternately holding my breath and exhaling on command, I was irradiated by a robot arm. Barbara, of course, was behind a lead shield.

Before the 1,343-acre burn with the aid of Nine-Five-Whiskey, we warmed up with a three-hundred-acre hand-lighting job. Our mission was to run brush-killing fire through a shrubby bog to preserve and enhance sedge grass habitat for sharptail grouse, sandhill cranes, and other birds. Contrary to the homilies of that hugely successful propagandist Smokey Bear, fire in the wild tends to be mostly beneficial, and a majority of the planet is a fire ecosystem to one degree or another.

Fire requires three ingredients: fuel, heat, and oxygen. This trio is dubbed the "fire triangle," and if any leg of the triangle is absent, a fire is impossible. The biosphere is carbon-based (fuel), the atmosphere is oxygen-rich, and lightning peppers the globe. The world wants to burn, likes to burn. Biodiversity thrives on fire. Ashes are minerals—nutrients, fertilizer—and black ground warms quickly.

We began on the windward flank of the site, lighting narrow strips of fire to back slowly into the brisk southeast wind away from our control lines. "Make it black" is the axiom. There's no better firebreak than freshly burned ground.

I started the show, grasping a drip torch in my right hand, pushing through alder and willow brush with my left. My rubber boots squished through saturated sphagnum and were soon brimming with water, but the surface fuels were crispy, and I was amused again by the notion of soggy feet and baked eyebrows. I gathered a Nomex shroud to my neck and face as I slogged ahead of the intense fire I was creating.

A drip torch is a handheld aluminum can with a spout and a wick, containing a mixture of fuel oil and gasoline. An internal breather tube controls the flow of fuel to the wick, and once lit, the flammable liquid is controlled by tipping the torch at various angles or by adjusting the breather tube opening with a set screw. I think of it as a magic wand. Poof! Fire: cleansing, liberating, life-renewing flames.

After my original strip of backing fire proved cooperative, other torches were lit, and soon we were ringing the west and north borders of the site with black. Our four Bombardiers followed up, patrolling for "slopovers" and aerial spotting across the lines. One spot fire did ignite. An ember from some heavier, woody fuels wafted over the line on an errant gust. It grew rapidly in dry grass on the west side, and three Bombardiers closed in like bugs to a lamp. My boss hustled to the spot, then called me on the radio: "Keep an eye on that corner."

I'd ceased lighting when I reached the southwest corner of the burn, awaiting the outcome of the spot fire and our suppression forces' redeployment along the lines. In a half-hour the spot was engaged, extinguished, and mopped up. A little fire outside the line is no disaster, but preventing it is a matter of pride. I kept an eye on that corner.

My boss returned, checked the wind, and was pleased. Conditions seemed right for the headfire, the main blaze to sweep across the site and complete the transformation, discouraging the encroachment of brush and forest into wetlands habitat.

"Ready?" he asked. I nodded. I'd just refilled my drip torch.

"Let's make some fire," he said.

"I can do that."

I dropped a match into a patch of brown grass, then shoved the wick of the torch into flame. It promptly heated and ignited.

With a ten-to-fifteen-mile-per-hour wind at my back and the lines to the west and north blackened, my task was to proceed as quickly as possible—induce a ripping conflagration.

I held the torch out and down, the flaming fuel mix dribbling freely from the spout, and strode away to the east. Given the breeze and a relative humidity of 25 percent, my impact was instant. Three-to-four-foot flames seemed to snap out of the earth and leap away to the northwest. In a minute, the headfire was rolling like a comber, with flame lengths of ten to twelve feet. This was a chain reaction unleashed, unstoppable—a significant, purposeful deed that could not be undone. Is that why I laughed with pleasure, intoxicated with power? Licensed to burn!

I humped through grass, moss, and brush for over a half-mile, laying down fire. At the southeast corner, beside a wet ditch that guarded our east flank, I sunk to my knees with an empty torch. Tired, yes, but also awed. "My" smoke, a convoluted, twisting plume, billowed to five thousand feet. It suffused my field of vision—like weather, like a swelling thunderhead, a gray-black cloud brindled with lanes of beige. *Mountainous*, I thought. It was a convection column, drawing all fire—west, south, east—into itself, and rotating slowly like an embryonic tornado.

We made that. We tended it; acolytes of the Vestal Virgins and disciples of Prometheus. I felt reverent. Back down the line, two of my colleagues were yelling, pointing at the column. *Yes, people, I can see it.* Anyone on a high spot within fifty miles could see it. *I made that.* Burn baby, burn.

My doctor told me: "OK, we'll do a blood test to make sure your kidneys are working normally. If they aren't, the IVP could push them into failure and you'd be on hemodialysis. I'll check the blood work, *then* we'll do the IVP. OK? Blood test first."

A few days later I arrived for the tests, and a nurse called my name almost immediately—no time for a *National Geographic* in the waiting room. Good. Let's get this over with. She escorted me down a hallway, bumped open a door with her hip, and I froze on the threshold. It was the X-ray room. What about the all-important blood test?

"Uh . . . ," I said.

She glanced at her clipboard. "You're here for an IVP, right?"

Language returned. "I'm supposed to have a blood test *first*. To see if the kidneys can take *this*." I flapped an arm into the room.

"Oh . . . " She seemed uncertain, but I spun on a heel and stalked out. *Keep an eye on that corner.*

Our third burn that week was a 3,990-acre site being scorched for the first time. The crew was excited but wary. We were familiar with the trouble spots on the others—been there, done that—but we might learn the hard way on fresh turf. As one firefighter put it, "no home-field advantage."

The big projects demand detailed planning and coordination. Besides Nine-Five-Whiskey and six J-7s, we had a mobile communications base with our own radio repeater and discrete frequencies, a medevac plan, safety officers, and weather observers. I expected a sixteen-hour day and lots of righteous toil. I stuffed a hefty lunch into my fireline pack.

Our division, a critical area on the south and east flanks, would be lit first. We had two J-7s and eight people, and with such a vast area to blacken, efficiency was paramount. We affixed an industrial propane cylinder and torch to one of the J-7s, aligning the nozzle so it ignited the fuels about a foot away from the treads. The J-7 operator worked the edge of the line and laid fire as fast as he could safely drive—five to ten miles per hour, depending on the track. A hoseman rode the back of the machine to snuff anything that tried to creep across the line.

My job was to hand-light a second strip of fire behind and parallel to the machine, about twenty yards out into the fuels.

This technique quickly established a wide and ever-expanding black swath in preparation for Nine-Five-Whiskey to start a headfire later in the day. Our second J-7 patrolled the rear.

Operations proceeded smoothly for the first hour, and we successfully burned around a cluster of historic log homestead buildings. We were initiating a long, two-mile drive to the north when one of the J-7s broke down. An awful grinding and slamming of gears in the front axle indicated it was out of the game. By the time a replacement arrived from another division, we were behind schedule, and picked up the pace. We knew we were lighting fast, but the fire remained manageable, so we pushed it. At one point the wind turned squarely and the flames swirled and arched the wrong way, but it lasted less than thirty seconds and seemed no big deal. I sucked a gust of dense smoke and trudged back to the line for a couple minutes of fresh air.

My radio crackled.

"Did you see that?" the boss asked.

"Affirmative, Tom; I was in it."

We advanced for another ten minutes, and I paused to take a swig from my canteen and check the line behind. There was a dark column of smoke about two hundred yards to the rear. I shoved the canteen back into its pouch and keyed my radio.

"Tom. You see that column behind us?"

A pause as he turned.

"Affirmative."

"I don't think it's on the right side of the line."

I started hustling back, and in a few moments I was sure it was on the wrong side.

"Tom. You'd better order that helicopter!"

"Ten-four."

One of our J-7s pulled up and I clambered aboard. As we hurried toward the spot fire I saw three or four mature balsam fir "torch out," that is, explode into tree-length flame. We had a major problem.

In a minute we were "on scene" and I hopped off the J-7. I was in my element. No one on our crew had more wildfire suppression training and experience than I (as opposed to prescribed fire management), and it was the chief reason I was temporarily on the Division of Wildlife payroll. It was implicitly understood that I should perform the size-up.

Marching through the black toward the head of the roaring fire, I was ebullient. I hadn't wished for things to go awry, but now that we owned this challenge, I wasn't unhappy. As Tom organized the J-7s and personnel to begin fighting up the left flank, I traversed smoking ground to the right, stepping through short flames on the edge of the blaze and skirting burning deadfalls. The heat was intense, but bearable, and I pulled my bandanna over my mouth and nose to filter smoke.

I estimated the spot at two acres, and in a few minutes I was in front of it. I crouched low into cooler, cleaner air, and looked around. I mean, really *looked*. It's easy to be seduced by adrenaline and torching trees, and not truly see what's happening—to overreact. *Concentrate*. I mumbled that under my breath. It helps to talk to yourself. I've explicitly advised rookies to prod themselves with audible reminders of what they know but can readily forget under stress.

I noticed three important trends:

1. Now that the fire was in the woods and partially shielded from the wind, the flame front was creeping, and had actually petered out in some areas.

2. This spot was now spreading by generating more spots. Torching conifers were casting embers ahead, and I saw three separate (tabletop-size) fires—no doubt there were more— but they were also anemic.

3. The prominent inferno was a "jackpot" of bug-killed fir, both down and standing; it was now well within the black.

So, unless we experienced a major increase in wind intensity, our chief problem was spotting, rather than running fire. First priority was to halt the propagation of spotting. Kill the jackpot.

I took a moment to rehearse a concise message to Tom, then keyed my radio. I couldn't break into the traffic. At that moment I heard Nine-Five-Whiskey come up on the second tactical frequency that was reserved for air-to-ground communications. He was enroute. I jumped onto that channel.

"Nine-Five-Whiskey. Leschak."

"Go ahead."

"Are you in touch with Tom?"

"Negative."

"OK, here's what we need to do."

I requested that his first bucket drops (one hundred gallons per shot) be directed on the jackpot of fuels and source of airborne embers before starting on the flanks and spots.

"Ten-four. Sounds good."

The pilot of Nine-Five-Whiskey was a virtuoso with a Bambi Bucket, and in less than ten minutes the main fire was reduced to smoldering logs and isolated pockets of flame. By then I'd reached Tom with my scouting report and we directed our ground forces to pinch off the flanks and hunt for more spots. Reinforcements were on the way. In a half-hour we were bumping from spot to spot, mopping up. I marshaled Nine-Five-Whiskey via radio and waving arms, and one by one the small fires were pounded with water drops. We had control.

And that was my joy: control. My radio was like a conductor's baton, influencing and manipulating information, machines, and people. From the instant I looked back and saw that wrong smoke until we left the spot cold and wet to resume lighting, I enjoyed a level of localized dominion that is rare in general, workaday life.

As we refilled canteens and drip torches, one of the wildlife specialists, new to suppression and still pumped up over the battle, slapped my arm.

"Hey, how did we do?"

I grinned. "We did fine, man, just fine." Fire tamers, by god; in control.

A month later, in late June, the fire season had long since been washed out by typically robust early-summer rains, and I was off the payroll. On the evening of June 27 the weathercasters saddled us with yet another severe thunderstorm and tornado watch, and by 10:30 P.M. it was upgraded to a warning. I strolled down to the lake to witness the maelstrom bearing down from the northwest.

The air was still warm, and the surrounding bog was glittering with fireflies. They darted and winked amidst a scattering of tamaracks and black spruce, and their silent mating signals were like a cheerful code of nonchalance against the dark. Their cool chemistry was counterpoint to the violent fireworks on the western horizon. The advancing storm was feverish with lightning. Jagged cloud banks were almost continually silhouetted with flashes and spikes. The thunder, still subdued by distance, was a constant rumble. A brisk southerly breeze rippled the lake. There was no calm before this storm. A bad sign—clashing frontal systems. No doubt the meteorologists were wise to warn us. It occurred to me that if not for the recent downpours, this lightning would ignite wildfires, slam me back on the payroll.

I savored the delicious apprehension sparked by such a juggernaut. There was no issue of control. I could not call on Nine-Five-Whiskey. Thunderstorms do not drip their fire, but lash it indiscriminately from the sky. You may be a target, you may not. I fear them more than I used to. In the past dozen years I've seen four homes set ablaze by downstrikes. In my capacity as the local volunteer fire chief, I had to deal with the aftermath, trying to gain control.

I thought about my medical tests. One more to go—at least for now—and still no indication whether anything was wrong. I felt like the fireflies before the storm, blinking away at life as if the night would remain peaceful. And why not? It seemed the appropriate way to behave.

When I saw sheets of backlit rain and the brawny arms of the front curving in, I retreated to the house. We had a little time yet, and I readied my fire department turnout gear—arranged my boots and bunker pants so I could easily step into them, and laid my radio next to the bed.

The storm struck at 11:30 P.M., so noisy and ominous that it was pointless to hope for sleep. Pam and I lay in bed, reading. Shortly after midnight a tremendous thunderclap rattled the windows. Our lamps went out, but the room was flooded with a brilliant flash of white light. There was a loud pop in the office down the hall.

For a moment I was frozen with fright; then I sprang out of bed and clawed at the nightstand for a flashlight. We rushed into the office and smelled acrid smoke. From past experience, we had a suspect: the answering machine. Four times we've lost them to lightning. We felt the paneling around the phone jack and power outlet. Cool. I hurried to the basement and checked the breaker box. One was tripped. I reset it and we had light upstairs. Meanwhile Pam had picked up a battery charger that sat next to the answering machine atop a metal filing cabinet. The bottom of the charger was blackened. Then we gaped at the cabinet. A spot the size of a dime was discolored, the finish vaporized by heat, and in the center the steel had melted. It looked as if the tip of a soldering gun had been pushed into the cabinet.

Back in bed, wide-staring-awake, I noticed my radio. I'd been concerned about being dispatched to somebody else's house, but we were the target. No control, and we were the target.

I wondered how many nascent forest fires, ignited by lightning, were being obliterated by the torrents of rain drumming on the roof.

CHAPTER THIRTEEN

WHIP

I knew a phoenix in my youth, so let them have their day.

W. B. Yeats

I was never much of a brawler. My last bona fide fight was at age twelve or thirteen, a brief backyard tussle with a buddy. There was no clear victor, and I don't recall the *casus belli.*

But prowess in hand-to-hand combat was highly prized on Minnesota's Iron Range, and I admired (and feared) those boys who could fight. The faces of rivals and enemies were meant to be havocked. Split lips, bloodied noses, loosened teeth, black eyes were badges of honor—for both winner and loser. There must always be both: victor and vanquished. I learned that the hard way.

During one winter-term week in a high school phy-ed class, we were taught the basics of wrestling, then paired up to compete. George, my opponent, was near my height and weight, and our match was a genuine battle. Tumbling and grunting, we smeared sweat across the mat, first me on top, then George, until he finally earned the advantage and pinned me. Our instructor-referee flopped to the floor—eye level with our tangled bodies—

to make sure my shoulders were down, then slapped the mat twice. Two seconds and out; George had beaten me.

But it was a fair fight, and as we rose to our feet I smiled and shook his hand.

"Nice going," I said.

The instructor bristled.

"You lost," he spat. "Losers don't smile."

He slipped his whistle from around his neck. It was tied to a knotted leather cord that doubled as a whip.

"Bend over," he said.

Yes, I "assumed the position"—hands on knees, bent at the waist. The whip snapped at my hamstrings, two vicious swipes. The pain wasn't excruciating, but physical hurt wasn't the point. It was about authority and humiliation. Everyone in the gym was watching.

I remember two clear thoughts as welts rose on the back of my thigh: *I'm being punished for smiling, for being a good sport*, and *this guy's an idiot*. I resisted the impulse to smile and say, "Hey, nice going." In retrospect, maybe I should've done it—enraged him, made him whip me again and again until he drew blood. How would he explain blood on the gymnasium floor to the principal? Well, disrespect and insubordination, no doubt. But I would reply, "Sir, I'm bleeding because I was smiling and offering a compliment. OK?"

Naw. Probably wouldn't have worked. The authority figure would've had more credibility, and besides, he was right: in our contemporary American culture, losers don't smile. Life is a zero-sum game in pursuit of money and material advantage, and you must vigorously clutch your slice of the pie. Nice guys finish last. In that context the instructor could have claimed his whistle-whip was a righteous appliance endorsed by the *Book of Proverbs*, a tool of the Almighty: "A father who spares the rod hates his son" (13:24), and "A whip for the horse, a bridle for the ass, and a rod for the fool's back" (26:3).

And how foolish of me to gracefully acknowledge defeat. I'm sure the instructor felt righteous. He looked smug. Several years later I read in Nietzsche, "Distrust all in whom the impulse to punish is powerful," and the instructor's face jumped to mind.

I was both angry and bemused after being whipped, but ultimately, grateful. The lesson: just because someone wields dominion (and force) doesn't mean they are right, moral, smart, or wise. That's important for a kid—inherently vulnerable—to understand. I accepted the whipping, but knew it was wrong-headed. I therefore ignored it as a personal censure. Besides, among my peers it was glory.

A few years before this episode, at a presidential press conference on March 21, 1962, John F. Kennedy said, "There is always inequity in life. Some men are killed in a war and some men are wounded, and some men never leave the country . . . . Life is unfair."

Not stunningly profound, and the majority of people who inhabit the planet have probably echoed that sentiment at one time or another. Considering the general tenor of human history and daily existence, it can hardly be debated. But in Kennedy's context—warfare—I'm one of those who never left the country. Only a portion of my many battles have been life-and-death, and the fact that I'm still here, relatively healthy, relatively content, testifies that I've not yet suffered horrendous loss, nor, obviously, the ultimate loss.

In some ways I've enjoyed a charmed life, and I cannot complain of blatant, purpose-crushing inequity. For the past forty-eight years it's been a fair fight. My goal in the warrior spirit is to embrace victory and defeat with the same mindset, that is, gratitude for the challenge, respect for the opponent. Realizing, of course, that the opponent is most often inside your own head. I still try to smile after losing a fair fight.

I'm not naive. I know my professed equanimity could evaporate tomorrow. The list of potential calamities is long; the opportunities for gross misfortune are legion. And in most cases I could credibly hold myself blameless for whatever evil I may sustain.

But here's what I want to do. On the brink of losing an unfair fight, perhaps on the desperate verge of vanishing—I want to smile.

If I don't, they can whip my corpse.